All my best,
Nancy Jackson

PHOTOGRAPHERS

HISTORY AND CULTURE THROUGH THE CAMERA

NANCY JACKSON

Facts On File, Inc.

Photographers: History and Culture Through the Camera

Copyright © 1997 by Nancy Jackson

Facts On File, Inc.
11 Penn Plaza
New York NY 10001

Library of Congress Cataloging-in-Publication Data

Jackson, Nancy, 1951–
    Photographers : history and culture through the camera / Nancy Jackson.
        p.   cm. — (American Profiles)
    Includes bibliographical references and index.
    Summary: Profiles eight men and women whose artwork serves as visual documentation
of critical events and cultural eras in American history during the nineteenth and twentieth
centuries.
    ISBN 0-8160-3358-7 (hb : alk. paper)
    1. Photographers—United States—Biography—Juvenile literature.
    2. Documentary photography—History—Juvenile literature.
    3. Photography, Artistic—History—Juvenile literature.
    [1. Photographers. 2. Photography, Artistic.]   I. Title.
    II. Series: American profiles (Facts On File, Inc.)
TR139.J33   1997
770′92′273—dc20
[B]   95-31386

Facts On File books are available at special discounts when purchased in bulk quantities for
businesses, associations, institutions or sales promotions. Please call our Special Sales Department in New York at (212) 967-8800 or (800) 322-8755.

Text design by Cathy Rincon
Cover design by Matt Galemmo

Printed in the United States of America

10 9 8 7 6 5 4 3 2 1

This book is printed on acid-free paper.

Contents

Introduction

"My husband is about to lose his reason," said Madame Louise Daguerre to a member of the French Academy of Sciences in 1831. "He has given up his art and carries on fruitless chemical experiments. At present he has the obsession to retain images fixed on metal plates. He has sold our possessions to buy chemicals and to build an apparatus."

The academy scientist visited the Daguerre home the next day. Instead of convincing the artist-inventor to stop, he said, "Continue with your experiments, and if you lack the funds I shall assist you myself."

A few years later Louis Jacques Mandé Daguerre perfected his invention: the photograph.

The principle of the camera has been known for centuries. Artists, architects, and inventors used a device known as a *camera obscura*, which at first was an entire room. An image of a landscape, a building, or anything else that was outside in sunlight could be projected through a tiny hole drilled in one wall of a completely darkened room and shown on the opposite wall.

Inventive individuals modified the camera obscura by adding a lens or a mirror and projecting the image onto a table so an artist could trace it. By the seventeenth century, the camera obscura was fashioned from boxes or tents and made portable. Adventurers traveled with these early cameras to make drawings of spectacular or exotic places.

Meanwhile, as properties of chemicals became known, scientists experimented with compounds that made metal or paper sensitive to light. They were able to capture images created by sunlight but could not make these images permanent. Many prominent scientists also combined the use of camera devices and light-sensitive chemicals.

It wasn't until the 1820s when the Frenchman Joseph Nicéphore Niépce was able to make a camera image permanent. But each image took hours to make and the image was the negative—dark where it should be light, and light where it should be dark. Niépce formed a collaboration with Louis Daguerre, a painter who actively experimented with cameras. After Niépce died, Daguerre refined their work enough to introduce the *daguerreotype*, a camera image made permanent on a piece of metal. When looked at in direct rays of sun, the shiny sheet of metal showed a negative image. A turn of wrist made the image positive, or appropriately dark and light.

The process became known as *photography*, from the Greek words *photo*, meaning light, and *graphy*, meaning drawing. Photography has continued to evolve ever since. Metal plates were replaced by paper and chemicals were refined. Camera lenses became sharper, and cameras became smaller, automated, and even electronic.

At first, photography was considered the product of a mechanical device rather than an art. Artists found it easier to copy photographs instead of having a sitter pose to have a portrait painted. Architects praised photographs for rendering details of buildings and other scenes. The public loved photographs because they brought pictures of presidents, royalty, celebrities, and faraway locations into their homes.

For a hundred years, photographers, artists, and gallery and museum directors quarreled over whether photography was an art. From the beginning, photographers used cameras to capture the beauty of a particular still life or landscape. Like painters and sculptors, they posed people in picturesque settings. They experimented with improvements in the photographic process. As cameras and film became more sophisticated, they took candid pictures and focused on recording events. Photographers produced such significant work that photography was finally accepted as an art.

Photography has always been a way of seeing. For every photograph, the photographer makes a choice to point the camera in a particular direction and focus on a specific subject. Photographers want other people to see a scene, event, mood, or personality the same way they do. If photographers are successful, viewers make emotional connections to the image.

Photographers can manipulate how they take photographs. Gordon Parks said he had learned how the camera can lie. "It all depended how its users chose to see things," he wrote. "They could wait for a pleasant smile or a frown to cover their subject's face before tripping the shutter. With deliberate intent, an extremely low angle could change a comely face into one of ugliness, and the most righteous human being could be made to look evil."

From the earliest daguerreotypes, photographers learned techniques of retouching. They could make someone's hair look better, they could erase an image, or they could add people or background. Edward Curtis was committed to depicting Native Americans before their cultures were extinguished. To achieve that, his printer sometimes deleted evidence of modern life. As photographic equipment became more refined, darkroom techniques allowed photographic printers to make exquisite prints that could be enlarged to cover a wall or reduced to the size of a postage stamp.

Photographers also use negatives and prints that haven't been retouched—known as *straight photography*—to provide a record of truth. These photographs can transform ideas about people, institutions, and relationships. Lewis Hine's images of five-year-olds working in mines showed the public that children were being exploited. Similarly, Dorothea Lange's pictures of drifters during the Great Depression were proof that governmental action needed to be taken. Photographs are the greatest resource of modern history to find out how people dressed or what their homes looked like, what happened at important events, or who first crossed the finish line.

Sometimes reality is so harsh the camera is used as a buffer between the photographer and the scene. When Margaret Bourke-White entered the German concentration camps, she used her lens as a shield against what she didn't want to accept. She said, "People often ask me how it is possible to photograph such atrocities. I have to work with a veil over my mind. In photographing the murder camps, the protective veil was so tightly drawn that I hardly knew what I had taken until I saw prints of my own photographs. It was as though I was seeing these horrors for the first time."

On their own they can make significant impact, but combined with words, photographs can become even more powerful. By the 1880s, photographs could be reproduced in newspapers and magazines. At first they were used only to illustrate articles. Soon they were used by manufacturers to catch the reader's eye in advertisements. Social reformers printed photographs in booklets they distributed to voters. Eventually, some publications used photos more prominently than words, as *Life, Look*, and other picture magazines gave America a look at itself and the world.

The United States has produced many master photographers who have made enormous contributions. The profiles in this book are a selection of just a few. Their lives span the history of photography and the exciting inventions that made it easier. Mathew Brady was 14 years old when daguerreotypes were invented. In his lifetime he saw photography change from taking long exposures on plates of metal to pocket cameras and roll film. By the time Edward Steichen was taking studio portraits of Hollywood idols, he was using sophisticated lighting and films that could capture motion instantly.

The photographers in this book recorded more than 150 years of American history. They took portraits of immigrants, soldiers, workers, farmers, presidents, wars, street life, and everyday life—and captured the face of history.

In the process, they made thousands of negatives and hundreds of photographic prints. Some of their most famous images are included in this book. Others can be found in books that focus on the work of individual photographers or books that contain photos of many photographers. Museums and galleries across the country display original photographs approved by the photographers themselves.

Each of these photographers achieved recognition while overcoming unique obstacles. Their lives are models of determination and inspiration. They had the ability to use their personalities with charm, bullishness, friendship, and understanding in a form that genuinely suited their feelings and purpose.

All of them depicted social conditions and the human spirit. As they focused on their subjects, the subjects became important, special. These photographers held a mirror up to truth. Because of their courage, they captured human dignity, despair, warmth, and hope, and in revealing the souls of others, they opened their own.

"One should really use the camera as though tomorrow he would be stricken blind," Dorothea Lange said. "Then the camera becomes a beautiful instrument for the purpose of saying to the world in general: This is the way it is. Look at it! Look at it!"

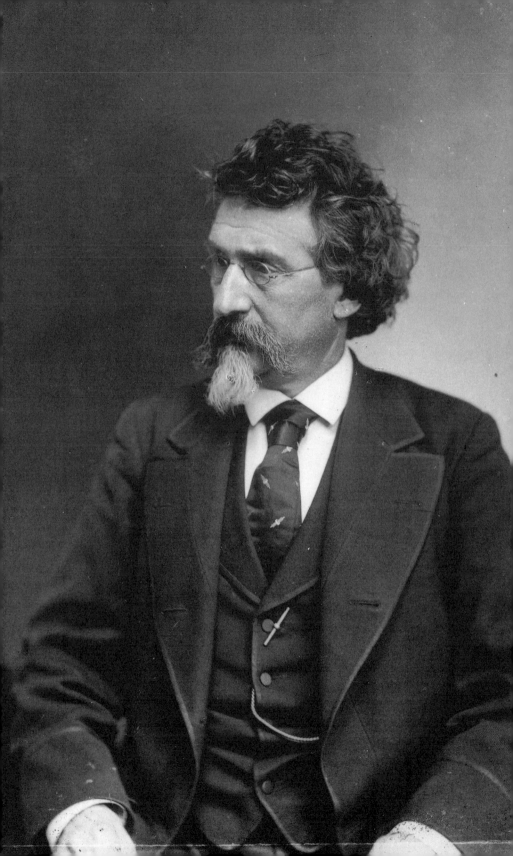

Mathew B. Brady

(1823?–1896)

In 1860, Mathew B. Brady moved his New York photography business into a huge and luxurious gallery. Located in a fashionable district at 785 Broadway and Tenth Street, it was resplendent. A colored skylight cast an emerald glow over rich upholstered furniture and a soft green carpet speckled with gold. Studio rooms could be reached by a private entrance so celebrities would not be crushed by admirers.

Brady's business was at its height. In 1851, he had received a grand prize for overall mastery of the medium at the World's Fair at the Crystal Palace in London. Since then he had built on his reputation for quality.

A variety of photographic processes had been popular for 20 years. But small photos called *cartes-de-visite*, French for calling cards, had

Mathew B. Brady, 1875, by Levin Corbin Handy (Brady's nephew). Writing about Brady's Civil War photographs, General Ulysses S. Grant said, "The collection will be valuable to the student and artist of the present generation but how much more valuable it will be to future generations." (Library of Congress)

just become a craze. The public clamored for pictures of singers, politicians, generals, and royalty so much that more than 300 million of these card photographs were sold each year. They were traded and collected, placed in photo albums, and proudly displayed in homes.

In autumn 1860, Edward, Prince of Wales and the son of Queen Victoria, arrived in New York. A parade and a ball commemorated the first American visit by a member of the British royal family. Brady was contacted to take the prince's portrait. On October 23, he closed his gallery to the public. Crowds of well-wishers cheered the royal party in their horse-drawn carriages, which stopped at Brady's National Portrait Gallery.

As he walked through the gallery, the prince inspected gilt-framed "likenesses." He would have seen life-size photographs and paintings of the U.S. president, James Buchanan; such authors as James Fenimore Cooper and Nathaniel Hawthorne; former First Lady Dolley Madison; world-famous showman Phineas T. Barnum; explorers; artists; and Brady's photographs of the presidential candidates, Stephen Douglas and Abraham Lincoln.

Brady asked the Duke of Newcastle, a member of the prince's party, why they had picked his studio. More than 70 other photo galleries competed for business in the city. The duke replied, "Are you not the Mr. Brady who earned the prize nine years ago in London? You owe it to yourself. We had your place of business down in our notebooks before we started."

Mathew Brady was born in 1823 or 1824 near Lake George, New York. His father, Andrew Brady, had emigrated from Ireland and most likely was a farmer. Mathew had four or five brothers and sisters. In later years, he signed his name Mathew with one *t*, and used the middle initial B with no indication of what it represented.

Not much is known about his childhood. But as a teenager, he traveled to nearby Saratoga Springs, perhaps to find a remedy for eye problems that grew worse as he got older. The famous resort community catered to a mixed clientele who sought the healing powers of the natural springs. There, he met William Page, a painter who encouraged Mathew's interest in art and gave him drawings to copy.

Brady was ambitious, even at an early age. When he was only 16, he accompanied Page to New York and took a job as a clerk at A. T. Stewart and Company, a department store. He learned how to make jewelry cases and soon opened his own business. By 1843, he was listed in a business directory as a jewel, surgical, and miniature case maker.

Page introduced Brady to his teacher, Samuel F. B. Morse, a painter and the president of the National Academy of Design. Morse had traveled to Paris in 1839 to get financial backing for his invention, a telegraph machine. There, he met Louis Daguerre, who later that year published his process of photography.

Daguerreotypes opened up the world of photography. Earlier photographs were either not permanent or took hours to expose. A daguerreotype was a permanent image that could be made in about 12 minutes of exposure. Advances in the next 10 years dropped the exposure time to 15 seconds, but even that can be a long time to hold a pose. In comparison, most daylight exposures today are taken at about 1/250th of a second.

Morse was fascinated by daguerreotypes and started giving classes in the difficult chemical process. Mathew Brady learned to take daguerreotypes from Morse, or from one of Morse's students.

The cameras were simple wooden boxes with a lens. They were held steady with tripods or other stands. People being photographed had to be carefully positioned. They were seated in an elegant chair or stood next to a column or table so they would look dignified. They might hold a book or be grouped in a family portrait. Their clothes had to be dark because light colors would turn into white blotches during the long exposures. Because the sitters had to keep perfectly still for a long time, the back of their heads were held tight in a clamp on a tall metal stand, called an *immobilizer*.

Taking a daguerreotype was a painstaking process that required many noxious chemicals. Brady learned how to cover a copper plate with silver and polish it until it gleamed. He would clean it in a solution of nitric acid. Then he would place the plate in a closed box and expose it to the vapor of iodine, which made it very sensitive to light.

As soon as Brady was satisfied with the pose and the focus on the lens, he carried the plate in a lightproof box to the camera, which was covered with a big black cloth. He placed the copper plate in a slot in the camera then removed the lens cap. Once a plate had been exposed to light, it was subjected to other chemicals that developed the image and "fixed" it, or stopped it from developing. Finally, it was thoroughly rinsed with water. The developing process generally took less than half an hour.

One-of-a-kind images, daguerreotypes made especially good portraits because they showed fine details. They were placed in a leather or imitation leather holder behind a piece of glass and purchased as mementos and gifts.

Brady bought cameras and chemicals. He practiced and taught others how to take daguerreotypes. Then in 1844, at the age of 21, he opened Brady's Daguerrian Miniature Gallery at 205 Broadway in New York City.

Because early photography required so much effort, a gallery owner directed the enterprise. From the start Mathew Brady decided his studio would be the finest. His silversmiths, artists, and clerks were paid well, and he hired the best camera "operators," as photographers were called. He supervised buying equipment and supplies and stayed current with technological developments.

Most important, Brady solicited business. "In those days, a photographer ran his career upon the celebrities who came to him," he said.

Brady became friends with influential people and invited politicians, artists, actors, writers, and speakers to have their portrait taken at his gallery—sometimes for free. Brady usually supervised posing the famous people. He used his charm to make them feel comfortable and encouraged them to send their friends. Because of his already poor eyesight, he allowed his camera operators to take most of the exposures. Yet all of the portraits in his gallery were credited to Brady.

One day in 1849, Edgar Allan Poe, the short-story writer and poet, came into Brady's studio with a friend, William Ross Wallace, who was having his daguerreotype made. Brady recognized Poe and asked him to sit for a portrait. "Poe rather shrank from coming, as if he thought it was going to cost him something," Brady said. He told

Edward, Prince of Wales, *1860, by Mathew Brady. Great Britain's crown prince gave Brady a carved walking stick to commemorate the occasion of his portrait. When Queen Victoria died in 1901, he became King Edward VII.* (Library of Congress)

MATHEW B. BRADY

Poe how much he admired him and his work, then explained there would be no charge, perhaps knowing he had no money. Poe sat and stared directly at the lens of the camera and revealed his determined personality, tinged with sadness. He died a few months later.

For those who could not come to his gallery, Brady had camera operators travel to them. He sent someone to take a daguerreotype of former president Andrew Jackson before he died, and Brady himself went to the White House to capture the image of President James K. Polk in 1849. Over his lifetime, Brady would have photographs made of more than a dozen U.S. presidents, from John Quincy Adams, the sixth president, to Congressman William McKinley, who became the 25th. Brady said, "From the first I regarded myself as under obligation to my country to preserve the faces of its historic men and mothers."

One of Brady's acquaintances was the great showman Phineas T. Barnum, who operated a museum across the street. Brady took daguerreotypes of many Barnum celebrities. The wildly popular singer Jenny Lind, known as the Swedish Nightingale, posed for Brady, as did three-foot-high Tom Thumb and his wife, and other acts in Barnum's show, including a bearded lady, Siamese twins, and a man so thin he was called the Living Skeleton.

It wasn't only the famous who had their pictures taken at Brady's gallery. From 1844 to 1854, approximately 300,000 people immigrated to the United States each year. The first stop for most immigrants was New York, the most populated city in the Western Hemisphere. Streets bustled with pedestrians and horse-drawn carriages. Residents and visitors would stop by Brady's gallery to have their "likeness" taken for a dollar or two. For an extra charge, an artist would color the daguerreotype with dry, powdered pigment to make the skin a more realistic color and to add color to the clothing or background.

"From the first I regarded myself as under obligation to my country to preserve the faces of its historic men and mothers."

In the United States, three million daguerreotypes were made in 1853 alone, and thousands of operators earned their living in the business. Brady made his gallery famous by covering the walls with daguerreotypes of the most celebrated people of the time. Unlike today's photography, where countless prints can be made from each negative, daguerreotypes were one-of-a-kind. But artists copied them in oil paints or made engravings.

Visitors would stop by the gallery to look at the portraits and have their own picture taken at the same time. They also could buy pictures of famous people. Because copyright laws had not yet included photographs, it was common practice to make copies and sell them—no matter who took them.

One of Brady's advertisements proclaimed: "Likenesses in all cases warranted to give satisfaction, and colored in the most beautiful manner by a practical and competent artist. Ladies, gentlemen, and all strangers are invited to call at the gallery, whether they intend sitting or not."

From the start, Brady entered his work in competitions. In 1844 he won prizes for the quality of his photographs from the American Institute of the City of New York and he continued to win for the next five years. He entered 48 of his best daguerreotypes in the 1851 World's Fair in London, competing with 700 pictures exhibited by photographers from six countries. Brady was awarded one of the five grand prizes for overall excellence.

Because magazines and newspapers could not reproduce daguerreotypes, they were copied by artists into different graphic media that could be printed. Two common types were lithographs, where the artist drew on a special stone that could be inked for printing, and engravings, which were usually etched or drawn on metal plates.

Such popular magazines as *Harper's Weekly* and *Frank Leslie's Illustrated Newspaper* used Brady as their primary source for illustrations. Readers got used to seeing the credit line, "from a daguerreotype by Brady," which brought in even more business. Brady said, "My gallery has been the magazine to illustrate all the publications in the land."

Brady decided to publish his own book of some of America's most prominent individuals. He had daguerreotypes taken of Presidents Zachary Taylor and Millard Fillmore. The great orator Daniel Webster sat for his portrait, as did the naturalist John James

Audubon. Brady hired an artist to make lithographs from the daguerreotypes. Published in 1850, *The Gallery of Illustrious Americans* was a beautiful book. But it had only 12 pictures of famous Americans and its $30 price was too expensive for most people. When sales of the first volume proved disappointing, Brady decided not to publish the second volume he had planned.

By the early 1850s, photography had gone through many improvements. Accordionlike bellows cameras were collapsible and easier to transport. A new process called *wet plate* was invented by the Englishman Frederick Scott Archer. In this process, a gooey liquid called *collodion*, and other chemicals, were used to coat a piece of glass to make it light-sensitive. The disadvantage of the wet-plate process was that the glass still had to be tacky or wet when the photo was taken. But glass was less expensive and easier to use than metal. Most important, each glass negative could produce innumerable positive images on paper. The glass negative was placed on a piece of sensitized paper and left in direct sunlight until the image appeared on the paper. Chemicals and water stopped the image from developing.

Methods of retouching photographs also had advanced. Artists enhanced images with oil paints, watercolors, India ink, charcoals, pastels, or crayon. They might erase some stray hair, smooth out wrinkles, or fill in the color of a coat or dress.

Once photos became easy and inexpensive to reproduce on paper, they were sold commercially on a vast scale as cards measuring 4 by 2½ inches. Seemingly, everyone had their pictures taken and left their photographic cards when they visited. They collected pictures of their friends and family and famous people they admired. They might visit Brady's gallery, browse through albums of sample photos, and buy copies of the ones they liked.

New cameras took two, four, or eight photos at a time. Operators reproduced pictures of famous people into the popular card photographs. Brady also supplied negatives of his collection to Anthony and Company, the largest American photo-supply firm, which also printed and distributed card photographs. Through this arrangement and his gallery, Brady sold tens of thousands of photographs a year.

Brady changed the location of his New York gallery twice. In 1853 he moved uptown to 359 Broadway and then in 1860 he moved to

M. B. Brady's New Photographic Gallery, Corner of Broadway and Tenth Street, New York, *1861, engraving by A. Berghaus. Brady's world-renowned portrait studio catered to the rich and famous and sold thousands of card-size photographs to the general public.* (Library of Congress)

the luxurious gallery at 785 Broadway. In 1849 he also opened a gallery in Washington, D.C. But other daguerreotypists ran well-established galleries there and Brady couldn't compete; he closed the Washington gallery a year later, then reopened it in 1858.

His accumulated wealth allowed Brady to enjoy the high life. In 1858, he married Julia Handy, a well-educated young woman he had met in Washington. Together they lived in posh hotels and went out dancing at night. They hosted parties and receptions for celebrities and politicians. Brady had become the most famous American photographer of the 19th century.

Meanwhile, two different societies had developed in the United States. By 1860, eighteen million people lived in the North, while nine million lived in the South. The North had natural resources, transportation, and most of the U.S. manufacturing. But the South provided cotton, which accounted for more than half of all American goods exported to other countries. About three million slaves sup-

> "I can only describe the destiny that overruled me by saying that . . . I had to go. A spirit in my feet said, 'Go,' and I went."

ported the cotton industry. Southern states relied on slave labor and had threatened to secede from the United States to preserve their way of life.

On February 27, 1860, Abraham Lincoln gave a rousing speech at the Cooper Union Hall in New York City. He voiced his conviction that slavery is wrong, but he emphasized that the North and South should live in harmony. He closed the speech with his famous words, "Let us have faith that right makes might, and in that faith let us to the end dare to do our duty as we understand it."

That day, he did something that would win him even more fame than the speech and the newspaper reviews that praised his eloquence. He went to Mathew Brady's portrait gallery to have his photograph taken.

In a new but rumpled suit, he allowed Brady to fix his collar and straighten his ribbon tie. He stood still while Brady placed the uncomfortable immobilizer on a stand to accommodate for his six feet four inches of height.

The photograph was reproduced as engravings in newspapers and magazines with articles about Lincoln as he continued to give speeches that spring. It was copied and pinned to ribbons after Lincoln was nominated that summer by the Republican party as its candidate for president of the United States. It was reduced to fit small half-inch medals people wore pinned to their clothes. The picture was also made into card photographs.

Never before had a presidential candidate been so visible to the public. A year later, when the newly elected President Lincoln went to Brady for another portrait, he said, "Brady and the Cooper Union speech made me president."

By then, Southern states had seceded from the Union. A month after Lincoln's inauguration as the 16th president of the United States, Confederate guns fired on the Union post of Fort Sumter in South Carolina. On April 15, President Lincoln called for 75,000 volunteers. During the Civil War, the Confederacy fought for independence. In order to destroy the opposing government, Northern armies had to invade the South.

Mathew Brady recognized the colossal significance of the event. He asked Lincoln to hire him as the photographer for the war. Lincoln would give him no money, but he wrote on a piece of paper, *Pass Brady. A. Lincoln.*

Years later, Brady said, "My wife and my conservative friends had looked unfavorably upon the departure from commercial business to pictorial war correspondence, and I can only describe the destiny that overruled me by saying that . . . I felt that I had to go. A spirit in my feet said, 'Go,' and I went."

Brady customized wagons to be used as traveling darkrooms. Built-in shelves and boxes held cameras, tripods, cloths, glass plates, and bottles of silver, iodine, chlorine, and other chemicals. The covered wagons were so odd the soldiers called them "what's it" wagons.

Like many who thought the war would be over quickly, Brady went forth on a hot July 21, 1861, to Bull Run, a stream near Manassas, Virginia. He took photos of men in their uniforms, in camp, and awaiting the conflict. He also took them after the battle, showing the dead and the wounded. The Confederacy won the Battle of Bull Run, and it was the start of the long, bloody war.

Brady returned to Washington, D.C., and made prints from his glass-plate negatives. He hung the pictures in his Washington, D.C., and New York galleries, and they were reproduced in newspapers. Brady was certain that people would want to buy photographs of the war, just as they had bought his photos of famous people and places. He also saw a place for himself in history.

Journalists and readers once again recognized Brady's leadership as America's premier photographer, especially when they read the credit line, "From a photograph by Brady." Meanwhile, thousands of soldiers had their photographs taken to give to family and friends at home. Many of them stopped at Brady's galleries and his business thrived.

During the four years of conflict, Brady spent more than $100,000 and ran up additional debt for supplies. He went to many battle sites. But mostly he relied on his staff of 20 camera operators and their

Cooper Union Portrait of Abraham Lincoln, *1860, by Mathew Brady. Lincoln made his position clear when he addressed a crowd of 1,500 people at the Cooper Union: "Even though much provoked, let us do nothing through passion and ill temper."*
(Library of Congress)

assistants to photograph the war. Although Brady took the credit, many of the most famous war photographs were taken by Brady camera operators Timothy O'Sullivan and Alexander Gardner.

Brady's war photographers endured the same challenges as the armies—crossing rivers and pulling wagons through rain and mud or dust and heat. They ran short of supplies, broke bottles of chemicals, and accidentally crushed the fragile glass-plate negatives. Their wagons made excellent targets for Confederate sharpshooters and were cumbersome during retreats.

Thousands of photographs recorded the fields of battle, artillery, bridges, and encampments. The American public saw the destruction and death created by the war. Brady made sure he had pictures of every type of soldier from drummer boy to general, including the presidents and commanders-in-chief, Abraham Lincoln and Jefferson Davis.

By the end of the war, the public had had enough. They didn't want pictures to remind them of the death and destruction they had endured. Card photographs were no longer popular and new business fell drastically. Brady also had been so involved in his war effort that he had let his own businesses run down. Yet he continued to spend lavishly.

Although Brady continued to operate his galleries, he was hounded by creditors. He declared bankruptcy and fled from New York authorities. In desperation, he proposed that the U.S. government purchase his entire collection of portraits and Civil War photos. He continued to badger officials until, in 1875, Congress appropriated $25,000 to pay Brady for clear title to 7,000 glass-plate negatives.

The money was not enough. He paid off some debts and kept operating, but by 1881, he had to close his gallery in Washington, D.C. From 1882 to 1894, however, he continued to work for or in partnership with others.

Brady's wife, Julia, died in 1887 and he lived with his nephew, Levin Corbin Handy, who also became a portrait photographer. On January 15, 1896, Mathew Brady died of a kidney ailment in New York City. He was buried in the Congressional Cemetery in Washington, D.C., where his tombstone is inscribed: *Renowned photographer of the Civil War.*

Chronology

1823?	Mathew B. Brady born near Lake George, New York
1839	moves to New York City
1843	manufactures jewel and daguerreotype cases
1844	opens Brady's Daguerrian Miniature Gallery
1849	opens gallery in Washington, D.C.
1850	publishes *The Gallery of Illustrious Americans*
1851	is awarded prize, World's Fair in London
1853	moves New York gallery to 359 Broadway
1858	marries Julia Handy; reopens gallery in Washington, D.C.
1860	moves New York gallery to 785 Broadway
1861	organizes photographic corps for Civil War
1868	declares bankruptcy
1875	receives $25,000 payment from U.S. government for his collection of photos
JANUARY 15, 1896	Brady dies in New York City and is buried in Congressional Cemetery in Washington, D.C.

Further Reading

Hoobler, Dorothy and Thomas Hoobler. *Photographing History: The Career of Mathew Brady.* New York: G. P. Putnam's Sons, 1977. Excellent young adult biography, illustrated with Brady photographs.

Meredith, Roy. *Mathew B. Brady's Portrait of an Era.* New York: W. W. Norton and Company, 1982. Adult biography by the author of several books on Mathew Brady and the Civil War.

Sullivan, George. *Mathew Brady: His Life and Photographs.* New York: Cobblehill Books, 1994. Excellent, illustrated, easy-to-read young adult biography.

Edward S. Curtis

(1868–1952)

" The sight of that great encampment of prairie Indians was unfor-
gettable," Edward Curtis recalled. "Neither house nor fence
marred the landscape. The broad, undulating prairie, stretching
toward the Little Rockies miles to the west, was carpeted with tepees.
The Blood and Blackfeet from Canada were also arriving for a visit
with their fellow Algonquin."

In Montana during the summer of 1900, Curtis witnessed the Sun
Dance, the most important ceremony of the Plains Indians. He was
only 32 years old. But during his lifetime, he had seen Native
American territories grow smaller. After the Civil War, the U.S.
government had escalated its war against the Indians, culminating in
the massacre of Wounded Knee in 1890, when more than 300 Sioux
died.

Self-Portrait, *1899, by Edward Curtis. Not surprisingly, everyone who worked with
Curtis called him "Chief."* (Special Collections, Division University of Washington
Libraries)

By 1891, the government had officially declared the frontier "closed." But many Indians still lived on their native lands—in the plains, the desert, and the Pacific Northwest.

As Curtis met with the Blackfoot Indians and photographed their leaders, he made a commitment to devote his enormous energies to create a permanent record of their faces for generations to come.

He said, " . . . It was at the start of my concerted effort to learn about the plains and to photograph their lives, and I was intensely affected."

Edward Sheriff Curtis was born to Ellen Sheriff Curtis and Johnson Asahel Curtis on February 19, 1868, near Madison, Wisconsin. Edward had two brothers and a sister. His father had been a Union army private and chaplain during the Civil War and after the war, the family moved to Cordova, Minnesota, where Johnson Curtis served as a preacher for the United Brethren Church.

To reach his congregation, Johnson Curtis made canoe excursions along the lakes and connecting streams. Edward loved to accompany his father and learned how to camp, cook, and handle canoes. A robust, enthusiastic young man, blond-haired Edward grew to 6'2".

As a teenager, Edward showed an interest in photography. Although he had no formal education past grammar school, he taught himself about photography and art through books. Following an instruction manual, he built his own camera using a lens his father had brought back from the war.

Photography had changed since Mathew Brady supervised his crew of camera operators during the Civil War. Cameras in the 1880s had built-in shutters and came in varying sizes, from a 14-inch × 17-inch large format to small hand-held cameras similar to those used today. A new *dry-plate* process allowed the glass plates used for making negatives to be prepared ahead of time. Dry plates required shorter exposure times than the older wet-plate process.

Edward worked for a year or two at a photography gallery in St. Paul, Minnesota, where he learned developing processes. Most likely he also gained experience retouching negatives and photographic prints by filling in spots with India ink, or etching to create highlights.

Edward's father's health had never been good after the Civil War, and as Edward grew older his family relied on him more. He showed great leadership abilities when, before the age of 18, he took a job supervising 250 workers on the Minneapolis, St. Paul and Sault St. Marie Railroad.

By 1887, Johnson Curtis moved to the Seattle, Washington, area where the climate was more mild than in Minnesota. Edward went with him. They built a log cabin on a homestead in the area that today is Port Orchard. Edward worked on neighboring farms, chopped trees, dug clams, and grew fruit and vegetables. Soon the rest of the family joined them, but Johnson Curtis died the next year and Edward and his 13-year-old brother, Asahel, had to support the family.

Edward Curtis continued to take photographs and bought a camera from a gold-seeker heading to California. An avid outdoors-man, Curtis would climb the local Cascade Mountains and make sharp, well-composed photographs of the picturesque landscape.

In 1891, Curtis borrowed $150 and formed a series of partnerships in the photography and photoengraving business. He learned how to engrave printing plates for reproducing photos and drawings in local publications and set up a photography studio to take portraits. His early photographs show highly developed technical and artistic skills.

He became an expert at using light to enhance a portrait, some-times creating a soft, luminous look and sometimes producing a dramatic effect by lighting half a face and leaving the other half in shadow. He also learned how to achieve a full range of tones—shades of gray from white to black—to make a photograph visually exciting. Curtis and one of his partners, Thomas Gup-till, entered 101 photographs of Seattle citizens in a contest and won the bronze medal from the 1896 National Photog-rapher's Convention. They were cited for excellent posing, lighting, and tone.

"*Good pictures are the result of long study rather than chance.*"

In 1892 Curtis married Clara Phillips and soon had an even larger household to support. Along with his mother, younger brother, and sister, he took on the responsibility for his wife and several of her relatives. His own three children—Harold, Florence, and Beth—were born in the 1890s.

During the first years of Curtis's photography studio, Seattle was a boomtown. Washington had become a state in 1889. Gold had been discovered in the Klondike, a region in the Yukon Territory in northwestern Canada. Miners flocked into the city as the last stop-off point before sailing North. The population of Seattle grew, and with it, the demand for professional photographers.

At the studio, Curtis produced wedding pictures and portraits and sold prints of his photographs of mountain scenery. On his jaunts around the Seattle area, he also took photos of local Indians.

Since awards enhanced a photographer's reputation, Curtis entered more competitions. He won awards from the National Photographic Exhibition in 1898 and 1899, including the grand prize for three Indian pictures. The Indian photos were part of an exhibition that toured Europe for two years and made the Curtis name even more visible within photographic circles. In 1900, he accepted the position of vice-president for the Washington chapter of the Photographers Association of Oregon. He was written about in such publications as the *Seattle Times* and the *Lewis and Clark Journal,* and he wrote for *The Western Trail* and later for *Scribner's* magazine.

Curtis continued to take hiking trips to photograph Washington vistas. He became an expert climber and particularly loved 14,410-foot Mount Rainier. He'd pack his heavy camera and glass plates and carry them with camping supplies. Then he'd set up his equipment and wait until the light was perfect. He said, "Good pictures are the result of long study rather than chance. . . ."

One evening during the summer of 1898, Curtis and an assistant had made camp at the 10,000-foot mark when he met a party of climbers. They were members of a government commission, including high-ranking officials of the United States Biological Survey and the Division of Forestry. One member of the climbing party was George Bird Grinnell, the editor of *Forest and Stream* magazine and an expert on Plains Indians. Grinnell was so impressed with Curtis

A Snake Priest, *1900, by Edward Curtis. Curtis was so accepted by the Hopi Indians that he was initiated as a Snake Priest. After he participated in the 16-day ritual, he wrote, "Dressed in a G-string and snake dance costume and with the regulation snake in my mouth I went through [the ceremony] while spectators witnessed the dance and did not know that a white man was one of the wild dancers."* (Library of Congress)

EDWARD S. CURTIS

and his photography that he recommended him for a scientific expedition the following summer.

The 1899 Alaska expedition was financed by Edward H. Harriman, who controlled the Union Pacific Railroad and was one of the wealthiest, most powerful men of the turn of the century. Curtis and an assistant traveled in an iron steamer with 124 other members of the team, including geologists, biologists, foresters, artists, taxidermists, and the ship's crew. The purpose of the trip was to document the last American wilderness and to collect specimens.

During the two-month voyage covering 9,000 miles, Curtis took photographs of the landscape and geological formations. On board the steamer, he would have heard Grinnell lecture on the Blackfoot Indians of Montana, where he had spent 20 summers. He also would have listened to presentations by the naturalist John Muir.

In the field, Curtis gained experience in techniques of interviewing. He watched some of the country's finest experts ask questions and encourage the Native Americans to speak to the researchers. He saw them make descriptive notes, take photographs, and gather masks, clothing, and totems for museums and private collections. They recorded Indian songs using a process invented by Thomas Edison. The sound was etched by a needle on a wax-coated cylinder about the size of a drinking cup.

Curtis also gained experience in the perils of fieldwork. He and his assistant were in a canvas canoe, closing in to photograph formations in Glacier Bay, Alaska, when ice broke away and the wave nearly swamped them into the frigid sea.

Harriman commissioned Curtis to make souvenir photo albums for all members of the expedition. The Alaska trip increased Curtis's reputation and he had photos published in *Camera Craft,* the leading journal of photography on the West Coast.

The following summer, Curtis accepted Grinnell's invitation to visit the Blackfoot Indian Reservation. Since he grew up in Minnesota, Curtis knew more about Native Americans than most people. Although portraits of Indians had been available since photographs were introduced to the mass market, the general public had little information about Native Americans. Some Plains Indians traveled around the country and participated as actors in wild West shows, which depicted them as either bloodthirsty savages or the end of a noble race of people. Tribes of the Southwest long had been visited by tourists, but few people could make the journey to the isolated desert reservations. Many people, including Edward Curtis, thought the American Indians were destined to disappear.

That summer, Curtis decided to photograph the Native Americans as they may have been before white culture intruded upon their lives. He wrote, "The passing of every old man or woman means the passing of some tradition, some knowledge of sacred rites possessed by no other; consequently the information that is to be gathered, for the benefit of future generations . . . must be collected at once or the opportunity will be lost for all time."

Curtis traveled to Arizona and New Mexico to photograph the Pueblo Indians, and for the next few years he traveled between his Seattle studio and Indian settlements throughout the West. Rather than photograph Native American life as it was at that time, he posed his subjects in front of cloth backdrops or against an open field. He would pay people to sit for him and reenact battles or dances. He saw their poverty but did not photograph it. Instead, he chose to portray his subjects as wise and spiritual, and their rituals as sacred and harmonious.

At that time, his Seattle studio was run by his brother, Asahel Curtis, and many members of his extended family worked there as photographers or assistants, in the darkroom, or mounting finished photographs. The studio sold a series of postcards of Indian subjects, scenic views, and the still lucrative portrait services. In 1904, Curtis hired Adolph Muhr to manage darkroom, and for the next 12 years Muhr applied his considerable skills to enhancing Curtis's negatives and making the most beautiful prints possible.

The more photographs Curtis took of the Indians, the more value he saw in his work. He envisioned a comprehensive and permanent record that would document the "vanishing race" for all time. *The North American Indian* would be 20 volumes, 300 pages each, with 75 full-page photographs and an accompanying portfolio of 36 larger size reproductions. Many of the photos would be printed following the photogravure process, in which an image was transferred to a copper plate and etched. The result was a high-quality reproduction

A Child of the Desert, *1904, by Edward Curtis. Early in his career, Curtis developed a distinctive style of portraiture that featured introspective poses and dramatic lighting.*
(Library of Congress)

that featured soft photographic tones. But to achieve his goal, Curtis needed a publisher and money for assistants, transportation, hotels, interpreters, and equipment.

A vital connection was made in 1904 when he was invited by President Theodore Roosevelt to take photographs of the Roosevelt family at their summer home in Oyster Bay, New York. Roosevelt had learned about Curtis after Curtis won a photography contest sponsored by *Ladies' Home Journal.* An outdoorsman himself, Roosevelt had spent several years in the Dakota Badlands. He liked Curtis and thought his plan to photograph the Indians commendable. He gave him a letter of recommendation that Curtis probably used to get an audience with J. Pierpont Morgan, then the richest man in America.

Morgan approved his proposal for the book series and gave Curtis an interest-free loan of $75,000 to cover expenses. They both expected a commercial publisher to embrace the project, but when none could afford the expensive undertaking, Morgan convinced Curtis to publish and market the book series himself.

Curtis was obsessed with his project, to the extent that all other enterprises supported his vision. In the field, he traveled by covered wagon or by boat, carrying several cameras and their glass plates, a motion picture camera, darkroom supplies, and a tent with an adjustable skylight used as a portable studio. He also brought equipment for making recordings, books, a typewriter, and files filled with papers pertaining to his lecture engagements and the books' publication—as well as camping supplies for himself and his assistants.

After a day's photography, Curtis would make one print from each good negative, which would be sent with the negative to Muhr, his darkroom manager. Muhr followed Curtis's special notations to retouch the photos. He added details or highlights to enhance objects in the scene, or he deleted anything that may have been part of white culture, such as hats, parasols, wagons, even entire backgrounds. Ironically, Curtis and Muhr left in rifles and horses, both of which had been originally introduced by whites but had by then become an integral part of the Indian legend.

Curtis crisscrossed Indian territories and traveled by train across the United States more than 125 times to meet with sales associates, clients, and the Morgan family. He wrote, "As to the effort I have put forth to do the work, few men have been so fortunate as to possess the physical strength I have put into this; and year in and year out I have given to the very maximum of my physical and mental endurance in my effort to make the work a worthy one."

The first volume came off the presses in 1907. In the foreword to the series, Roosevelt wrote, "It would be a veritable calamity if a vivid and truthful record of these conditions were not kept."

Librarians and book collectors from across the country praised the work as exquisitely beautiful and an excellent record of Native Americans. An ongoing controversy surrounded Curtis's accuracy of facts and choice to pose his subjects rather than document them in action. But he later paid Frederick Webb Hodge, an expert at the Bureau of American Ethnology, to edit the books before publication, and criticism diminished. Initial sales were not as high as Curtis had hoped. Besides his large extended family to support, he had his field staff, workers at his studio in Seattle, and publishing and sales staff in New York and Boston. Curtis expended a great deal of his energy in fund-raising campaigns.

Through the years, he lectured in major American cities and showed slides of his Indian subjects. After one particularly successful presentation in Seattle in 1906, he said, "Last night I gave a stereopticon picture talk at the Century Club. The room was crowded. . . . The audience was as a whole breathlessly quiet, but occasionally cheering a picture. When the last picture went on the screen and I thanked them feelingly for their interest . . . the whole roomful of men rose to their feet with a cheer of thanks. . . . When a gathering like that will show such enthusiasm one cannot help but feel that he is right in the work."

Curtis developed a multimedia event that eventually was called *The Curtis Picture Musicale.* The presentation had motion picture clips of Indian dances; hand-tinted slides of chiefs, warriors, women, and artisans; and a 22-piece orchestra playing music based on wax cylinder recordings of Indian instruments and song. By the time Curtis brought it to the East Coast, the musicale played to capacity audiences in Boston and New York, including Carnegie Hall. He had expected to raise funds for his book project, but the musicale was too costly to produce and he stopped presenting the show.

"For every negative that is a disappointment there is one which is a joy."

He had successful exhibitions of his photographs in New York, Washington, Boston, and Pittsburgh. The Curtis pictures reflected the popular image of the noble Indian, and his idealized photographs were at the height of fashion. Curtis was admired in photography

At the Water's Edge—Piegan, *1910, by Edward Curtis. The idyllic life of the Plains Indians was romanticized in a picturesque encampment at the water's edge.* (Library of Congress).

EDWARD S. CURTIS

and art circles for what was called pictorial photography. His prints detailed the textures of skin, hair, beads, feathers, and other natural objects in a range of tones. They also evoked emotions of longing for an idyllic time that has passed and, for some, guilt that white culture had taken this away.

To raise money to support his Indian photography, Curtis decided to make motion pictures. He organized the Continental Film Company in 1910 and over the next few years filmed a docudrama of the Kwakiutl (pronounced kwock-ee-OO-til), a tribe in the Pacific Northwest. He researched the culture and discovered that in the past, the Kwakiutl had a custom of warriors taking the heads off the dead after battle. He called his film *In the Land of the Head-Hunters,* mostly because the title might entice the public.

"These people were seagoing, hardy, fearless, living on one of the most stormbound coasts of the North Pacific," he said. "The resulting habits gave me an opportunity for such picturesque effects as no other primitive tribes could furnish, for the war canoes of these Indians were as notable as the Roman galleys ever were. And a few of the originals remained to be used before my camera."

The silent film was a combination of fact and fiction. The story was contrived but scenes of authentically costumed dancers in their war canoes were spellbinding. Released in 1914, the film was well received by audiences and critics but never got the distribution it deserved, nor made any profit for Curtis.

By 1916, Curtis had published volume 11 of his North American Indian series. He also had written two other books, *Indian Days of the Long Ago* and *In the Land of the Head-Hunters.* For more than 10 years, his projects had taken him away from his family. The financial strain and the stress of running the studio finally were too much for his wife, and she filed for divorce. Their battles over money and property lasted for years.

Curtis moved south to Los Angeles. He opened a new studio in 1919 with his daughter, Beth, who had managed the Seattle studio for a number of years. While he continued making prints and writing his Indian books, Curtis worked on such films as Cecil B. deMille's *Adam's Rib, The Ten Commandments,* and *King of Kings.* He was a motion picture camera operator and also took still photographs.

Distinguished from moving pictures, still photos are taken of the sets and actors and used as reference for filmmakers while making a film, and for publicity.

During the 1920s and 1930s, Curtis also became a gold miner. Harold Curtis, his son, had a degree in mining engineering and worked in Colorado gold mines. Edward Curtis took a correspondence course in metallurgy and mining and patented a device that extracted gold using mercury.

By the time Edward Curtis and his daughter, Florence, once more traveled north to complete volume 20, he was tired. He limped from old injuries, and he had long before lost financial backing for his project. Still, he rented a small schooner and sailed through the icy seas for one last voyage along the coast of Alaska and the Bering Sea. Volume 20 was published in 1930.

During more than 30 years of photographing Native Americans, Edward Curtis took 40,000 exposures of individuals in 80 tribes. He recorded 10,000 songs and 75 languages. He raised more than a million dollars to add to the Morgan family contributions and he produced 291 sets of *The North American Indian,* which sold for $3,000 to $4,500 each.

By the 1930s, photographs of Indians were no longer in fashion. Curtis's documents were relegated to libraries and, disappointed, he died of a heart attack on October 19, 1952, in Los Angeles. But the 1960s brought a revived interest in Native Americans. His photographs—known as the "Curtis Indians" for their pictorial style—rose in value, and by 1993 one set sold for $622,500.

Curtis Indian portraits were also reproduced in books and magazines and used as research for films that recognized the vital contributions of Indians. Edward Curtis left an indelible stamp on the legacy of American culture.

"For every hour of misery I could tell you of one of delight," he wrote, "and the most stormy days have had glorious sunsets, and for every negative that is a disappointment there is one which is a joy, and for every page of these trials I could write you countless ones of the beauties of Indian-land and Indian life."

Chronology

FEBRUARY 19, 1868	Edward Sheriff Curtis born in rural Wisconsin
1887	moves to Seattle with father
1891	opens photography and photoengraving business
1892	marries Clara Phillips
1896	wins medal from National Photographer's Convention
1898	exhibits first photographs of Indians
1899	photographer for Harriman expedition to Alaska
1900	makes full commitment to photographing Indians
1904	meets President Theodore Roosevelt, who supports his endeavors
1905	exhibits photographs in East Coast cities
1906	J. P. Morgan finances *The North American Indian* book project
1907	Curtis publishes volume 1 of *The North American Indian*
1910	produces multimedia *Curtis Picture Musicale*
1914	releases film *In the Land of the Head-Hunters*
1919	moves to Los Angeles
1923	works as still photographer and camera operator for Hollywood movies
1930	publishes volume 20 of *The North American Indian*
OCTOBER 19, 1952	Curtis dies in Los Angeles

Further Reading

Curtis's Books
The North American Indian. 20 volumes.
Vols. 1-5, Cambridge, Massachusetts; vols. 6-20, Norwood, Connecticut, 1907-1930. Reprint. New York: Johnson Reprint Corporation, Harcourt, Brace, Jovanovich, 1978. Curtis's fascinating series of books about the daily life of American Indians in the early 1900s.

Books About Edward S. Curtis
Boesen, Victor and Florence Curtis Graybill. *Edward S. Curtis: Photographer of the North American Indian.* New York: Dodd, Mead & Company, 1977. Well-illustrated, easy-to-read, young-adult biography coauthored by Edward Curtis's daughter.
Davis, Barbara A. *Edward S. Curtis: The Life and Times of a Shadow Catcher.* San Francisco: Chronicle Books, 1985. Comprehensive coffee-table book about Curtis's life, filled with photographs.

Alfred Stieglitz

(1864–1946)

"On Washington's birthday in 1893, a great blizzard raged in New York," Alfred Stieglitz later recalled. "I stood at the corner of 35th Street and Fifth Avenue, watching the lumbering stagecoaches appear through the blinding snow and move northward on the avenue. The question formed itself: Could what I was experiencing, seeing, be put down with the slow plates and lenses available? The light was dim. Knowing that where there is light one can photograph, I decided to make an exposure."

No one had ever successfully taken photographs in the snow before. That afternoon, Stieglitz kept his equipment as dry as possible while he spent six hours in the freezing cold, photographing the exact moment when all the elements of action, light, texture, and tone merged to create the perfect image.

Self-Portrait, *1907, by Alfred Stieglitz. Intense and personable, Alfred Stieglitz helped bring photography into the ranks of art.* (Collection of the J. Paul Getty Museum, Malibu, California)

Later, even before the negative was dry, he showed it to fellow members at the New York Society of Amateur Photographers. One of his associates urged him to throw it away because, he said, "It is all blurred and not sharp."

"This is the beginning of a new era," Stieglitz replied. "Call it a new vision if you wish. The negative is exactly as I want it to be."

Twenty-four hours later when he showed a slide of the photograph, he received applause. "No one would believe it had been made from the negative considered worthless," he said.

Winter, Fifth Avenue was Stieglitz's most exhibited, reproduced, and award-winning print.

Alfred Stieglitz was an artist. As a photographer, he began establishing his reputation when he was still a college student. As a publisher, his magazines won international acclaim. As a gallery manager, he brought such European artists as Auguste Rodin and Pablo Picasso to the American audience and introduced the world to the artist Georgia O'Keeffe.

Most importantly, Stieglitz lived the life of an artist. His family and wealthy patrons supported his work in producing and promoting photography as fine art. He devoted his career to the exploration of the artist's role: to create, to innovate, to express feeling, and to share a vision of life.

He wrote, "I was born in Hoboken. I am an American. Photography is my passion. The search for truth my obsession."

Alfred Stieglitz was born January 1, 1864, the oldest of six children. His father and mother, Edward and Hedwig Stieglitz, had emigrated from Germany to New Jersey. Alfred's father was an amateur painter. He also was a successful businessman who owned and operated a highly profitable woolen business. The Stieglitz home was often filled with artists, musicians, and other interesting people who stopped by to socialize.

When Alfred was seven years old, the Stieglitz family moved to 14 East 60th Street in New York City. Although his family treated him as though he were frail, Alfred actually was very active. He enjoyed the still open spaces in New York and developed himself as a runner. Summers were spent at Lake George, New York, where Edward Stieglitz eventually purchased a house and more than five acres of land. Young Alfred—he was called Al—and the other Stieglitz children rowed, swam, and played tennis and billiards. He would spend every summer of his long life at Lake George, except for when he was in Europe.

From 1879 to 1881, Alfred attended the College of the City of New York. But, as all the Stieglitz children were getting older, his father wanted to be sure they received what he considered the best education. In 1881, Edward Stieglitz retired from his prosperous business and took the family to Germany. Alfred was expected to earn a degree in mechanical engineering and enrolled in the Berlin Polytechnic.

One day in 1883, Alfred Stieglitz was walking along the street in Berlin when he stopped at a shop that displayed a camera in the window. For the equivalent of $7.50, he came out with a camera, photographic plates, chemicals, and an instruction booklet. He already was familiar with photographic printing from watching photographers who had taken pictures of his family when he was growing up.

Once Stieglitz got his camera, he was obsessed by it. He constantly experimented with different chemicals and paper. He would scout out a place in the city or countryside and return time and again until the light was perfect. He also would photograph the same subject over and over to determine how light, exposure, and developing affected the image.

The Polytechnic had excellent photographic laboratories. Stieglitz volunteered to be responsible for them so he could spend day and night with his experiments. He also took classes from Dr. Hermann W. Vogel, who wrote for and edited publications about photography.

"I did nothing according to rote," Stieglitz said, "nothing as suggested by

"*Photography had become a matter of life and death. I worked like one possessed.*"

professors or anyone else. It is difficult to understand at this date the passion and intensity I poured into photographing during those early hours, days, weeks, and months! Photography had become a matter of life and death. I worked like one possessed, even though before long I ran up against a world not ready for true photographs."

He stopped taking engineering courses but sat in on classes given by well-known and inspiring lecturers. His father agreed to support his photography and gave him an allowance. Throughout the rest of the 1880s, Stieglitz lived in and traveled around Europe. He attended plays, musical concerts, and operas, and played the piano himself. He also spent hundreds of hours studying art in galleries and museums. Most of all, he carted his heavy photographic equipment from cities to mountaintops.

Like other photographers of the time, Stieglitz sought out picturesque landscapes, idyllic peasant life, children playing, or city life. His purpose was to capture the mood of a scene. He believed a good photograph should convey feeling.

During this time he began to publish articles about technical aspects of photography, he had photos displayed in galleries, and he entered competitions. In 1887 he received the first and second prizes from a contest sponsored by the publication *London Amateur Photographer*. He was pleased with the recognition and was inspired to work even harder.

Since photography had been invented in 1839, discussions raged about whether it was art. Some felt that excellent photographs were as good as the best drawings, paintings, or sculpture and rightfully belonged in museums. Most felt that photography was merely a mechanical process and could never be compared to fine art.

Stieglitz said that artists told him they envied his photographs but did not consider them art. He said, "Then and there I started my fight, or rather my conscious struggle for recognition of photography as a new medium of expression, to be respected in its own right, on the same basis as any other art form."

In 1890 when he was 26 years old, his father asked Alfred to return to the United States to get started in business. He offered him money to start a photography studio, but the young Stieglitz refused. Commercial photography—never! So the elder Stieglitz set him up

Sun Rays—Paula, Berlin, *1889, by Alfred Stieglitz. As a student, Stieglitz already had mastered the technical aspects of a good photograph—a pleasing composition, an interplay of light, and a variety of shapes and lines. He also reproduced the woman's quiet, relaxed mood.* (National Gallery of Art, Washington, D.C., Alfred Stieglitz Collection)

ALFRED STIEGLITZ

in the photoengraving business with two school friends, Joseph Obermeyer and Louis Schubart. Pressured by his family to marry, Stieglitz became engaged to Obermeyer's sister, Emmeline, and married her in 1893. Never interested in commercial enterprise, Stieglitz left the photoengraving business in 1895.

In the late 19th century, photographic equipment became easier to use. George Eastman had invented a camera with shutter speeds fast enough that it could be held by hand instead of mounted on a tripod. He also had invented film on a roll, similar to what we use today. Many photographers still used glass plates, however, because they felt they could get larger negatives and more details.

Thousands of hobbyists pursued photography. They joined together to form camera clubs, which provided darkrooms and libraries, lectures, and discussions about techniques of photography. In the United States, over 150 clubs boasted more than 5,000 members by 1895.

Stieglitz already had been a member of the Berlin German Society of Friends of Photography, and in 1891 he joined the New York Society of Amateur Photographers. The word *amateur* then was used in the strict sense of a person who pursued a hobby for love, not for money. Art photographers prided themselves in their amateur status. Stieglitz became the editor of the society's publication, *American Amateur Photographer* in 1893.

A few years later the society merged with the New York Camera Club. Stieglitz took over editorship of their publication, *Camera Notes.* He transformed it from a newsletter to a quarterly magazine of more than 200 pages. He later admitted, "I had a mad idea that the club could become the world center of photography and eventually create a museum. If only others had felt as I did, wonders could have been accomplished."

Stieglitz developed a high standard for the publications. To him, a photograph had to be technically excellent. It also had to meet his artistic standards by being pictorially interesting. Pictorial photographs created a mood or impression, told a story by catching a moment of time, or were poetic visions.

Stieglitz himself became the most visible and praised American photographer. Well on his way to an international reputation, by

Winter, Fifth Avenue, *1893, by Alfred Stieglitz. As equipment improved, Stieglitz became one of the pioneers of action photography and captured the powerful energy of these horses being driven through New York City snow.* (Library of Congress)

1902, Alfred Stieglitz had received more than 150 awards for his photographs. Through all kinds of weather, day and night, he would walk the streets of New York, looking for subjects to photograph.

He said, "I loved the signs, even the slush, as well as the snow, the rain and the lights as night fell. Above all there was the burning idea of photography, of pushing its possibilities even further."

ALFRED STIEGLITZ

In 1898, his daughter Katherine was born. Stieglitz and his wife, Emmy, had moved several times, and finally moved into a house owned by his brother, Leo Stieglitz, who was a doctor. Even though they had a live-in nurse, Emmy was nervous about taking care of their daughter and relied on Alfred to make decisions. She never understood his passion for photography or his commitment to art, and their marriage was distant. She may also have felt that he didn't maintain the lifestyle she wanted. They lived on money provided by his father and, later, by her brothers.

As he got older, Alfred Stieglitz became more opinionated. He chose photographers who shared his point of view about photography to include in club exhibitions and in the magazine. Many club members felt excluded from the Stieglitz-dominated club.

Meanwhile gallery owners and curators throughout Europe increasingly asked Stieglitz to send American photographic work he felt to be significant. He sent the finest prints from his stable of photographers, which were well received as the American school of photography.

Late in 1901, he accepted a request from the National Arts Club of New York to organize an exhibit, which he titled "American Pictorial Photography Arranged by the Photo-Secession." Stieglitz made up the term *photo-secession.* He had been familiar with a European painters' group that called themselves the Secessionists, because they seceded, or drew away from the rigid rules of painting at that time. Stieglitz called his group of photographers the Photo-Secessionists, meaning they were breaking the rules and founding a new style of art. The loosely organized Photo-Secessionists included such photographers as Clarence White, Gertrude Kasebier, and Edward Steichen, and eventually numbered more than 100 members.

Stieglitz organized Photo-Secession exhibitions in the United States and abroad. They were very popular with the public; more than 4,000 people attended an exhibition at the Corcoran Art Gallery in Washington, D.C., during the 12 days of the show, and in Pittsburgh, 11,000 came to a Photo-Secession exhibition. The Photo-Secessionist movement culminated in 1910 at the International Exhibition of Pictorial Photography at the Albright Art Gallery in Buffalo, New York. More than 15,000 people walked through the gallery space, which showed nearly 600 prints. The Albright was the first museum in the United States to buy photographs as art.

In 1903, Stieglitz started a new publication, *Camera Work*, which was published on the finest papers with the highest technical standards. He and other volunteers physically glued in the photographs, a process called hand-tipping. Like *Camera Notes*, the journal had reviews, articles on photographic criticism and techniques, and writings in philosophy, literature, and the arts. Through the 15 years of its publication, Stieglitz estimated he personally mailed out 35,000 copies.

Although he was kept busy to the point of exhaustion, Stieglitz continued to pursue his own photography. On a summer voyage to Europe in 1907, he took his famous image *The Steerage*. He and his family were in first-class accommodations, but walking around the ship, he spotted the composition for a perfect photograph of people crowded in steerage.

> The scene fascinated me; a round straw hat; the funnel leaning left, the stairway leaning right; the white drawbridge, its railing made of chain; white suspenders crossed on the back of the man below; circular iron machinery; a mast that cut into the sky, completing the triangle. I stood spellbound for a while. I saw shapes related to one another—a picture of shapes, and underlying it, a new vision that held me: simple people, the feeling of ship, ocean, sky, a sense of release that I was away from the mob called rich.

Stieglitz ran back to his cabin to get his camera and amazingly, the scene hadn't changed when he returned. "Some months later, after *The Steerage* was printed, I felt satisfied, something I have not been very often," he said. "Upon seeing it when published, I remarked: If all my photographs were lost and I were represented only by *The Steerage* that would be quite all right."

Along with exhibitions elsewhere, Stieglitz opened the Little Galleries of the Photo-Secessionists at 291 Fifth Avenue in 1905. Later the gallery became known just as 291. As collectors began to acknow-

The Steerage, *1907, by Alfred Stieglitz. Millions of Europeans immigrated to New York on large passenger ships and bought the cheapest passage known as steerage.* (Collection of the J. Paul Getty Museum, Malibu, California; photogravure size 13 3/16 x 10 3/8 inches)

ledge the value of photographs, many prints sold. Stieglitz himself bought prints and eventually built up a large, valuable collection.

It was as gallery manager that Alfred Stieglitz came into his own. His magnetism drew artists, critics, and influential members of society. He encouraged discussion and argument and earned a reputation for being generous and arrogant, welcoming and rude, caring and offensive—but always passionate.

The photographer Edward Steichen recalled, "His patience was almost unbelievable. With only a brief interruption for lunch, he stood on the floor of the galleries from ten o'clock in the morning until six or seven o'clock at night. He was always there, talking, talking, talking; talking in parables, arguing, explaining. He was a philosopher, a preacher, a teacher, and a father-confessor. There wasn't anything that wasn't discussed openly and continuously in the galleries at 291. If the exhibitions at 291 had been shown in any other art gallery, they would never have made an iota of the impact that they did at 291. The difference was Stieglitz."

The galleries originally only displayed photographs. Stieglitz first began showing paintings and drawings in 1907. Edward Steichen, then living in Paris, met with many artists who were innovators and leaders of a new movement known as *avant-garde*. Stieglitz was the first to display the works of now-famous artists Pablo Picasso, Henri Matisse, Auguste Renoir, Paul Cézanne, and Henri Toulouse-Lautrec. He also exhibited Japanese prints and African carvings. The public reacted with glee or outrage at the new and exciting style of art, and his shows paved the way for modern European and American painting and the public's acceptance of abstract art.

Stieglitz started another magazine, *291,* in 1915. He stopped publishing both *Camera Work* and *291* a few years later. He produced

> "*Often I have not, myself, completely understood what I have exhibited, at the very first. But if the spirit of someone's work has meant something to me, I have shown it in order to see for myself what living with it might disclose.*"

one more magazine, in 1922, a literary publication called *MSS,* which is the abbreviation of the word *manuscripts.* Each successive publication was called the most sophisticated American magazine of its day and had European imitators.

From 1914 through 1918, Europe was involved in World War I. Although the United States did not enter the war until 1917, the conflict heavily influenced American life. Other American galleries now displayed the work of the moderns. The era of the Photo-Secessionists was over, and when the building was scheduled to be demolished, Stieglitz closed 291.

In 1916, he met Georgia O'Keeffe. A friend of hers had brought him some O'Keeffe drawings, which he exhibited in his gallery. By 1918 he had left his wife and moved in with O'Keeffe. They were married in 1924 despite the 23-year difference in their ages.

His relationship with O'Keeffe invigorated Stieglitz, and he did a series of photographs of her. He had always been interested in exploring the human body as abstract art. She posed for more than 500 photographs—standing next to her paintings, in stark contrast to the sky, or in close-up, showing the crook of her elbow or her hands in a gesture.

Stieglitz also did a series of photographs of clouds that showed nature in even more abstract form. Just as in his student days, he would make a hundred prints of one negative until he got the perfect print. He converted bathrooms into makeshift darkrooms and would wash prints in a bathtub and hang them on a kitchen or attic clothesline to dry. One-man shows of his photographs in 1921 and again in 1932 received critical acclaim. Stieglitz was still at the top of his profession as an art photographer.

The public continued to look to Stieglitz for the newest in art and artists. His supporters convinced him to continue his exhibitions. From 1917 to 1925 he used rooms at the Anderson Galleries to promote the work of a select group of American artists. He managed The Intimate Gallery from 1925 to 1929 and An American Place until his death in 1946. Most often he showed paintings, drawings, and watercolors by Georgia O'Keeffe, Arthur Dove, John Marin, Marsden Hartley, and Charles Demuth, his own photographs, and those of Paul Strand.

Despite all of his achievements, Stieglitz still had not been able to get a major American art museum to include photos in their collection. Finally, in 1923, the Museum of Fine Arts in Boston asked Stieglitz to donate a group of his prints. Five years later, the Metropolitan Museum of Art in New York acquired Stieglitz photographs to add to their permanent collection. In 1933, he donated to them the collection of photographs he had purchased from other artists.

At the age of 73, Stieglitz felt he could no longer do the intense work of taking photographs and spending hours in the darkroom. He stopped his own photography. But that didn't stop him. His relationship with his wife, Georgia O'Keeffe, became long distance as she spent more time in New Mexico. But they always remained very close. His summers were still spent at Lake George with his extended family, which now included many nieces, nephews, and their children, who remembered him as eccentric but fun-loving Uncle Al.

During the winter season, he dressed in his usual salt-and-pepper suit, put on his cape and porkpie hat, and went to his gallery every working day. He especially enjoyed the white walls and graciously made himself available to all visitors. There, he continued the perpetual dialogue he had started back in his student days—the choices of each person's life and an investigation into truth, beauty, and art.

Alfred Stieglitz died July 13, 1946, in New York.

Chronology

JANUARY 1, 1864	Alfred Stieglitz born in Hoboken, New Jersey
1879	studies at College of the City of New York
1881	studies in Berlin, Germany
1887	wins first prize in photography contest
1890	owns and operates photoengraving business with two partners
1893	edits *American Amateur Photographer*, marries Emmeline Obermeyer
1897	edits *Camera Notes* and begins to organize and judge national and international photography exhibitions
1902	founds Photo-Secessionists
1903	edits and publishes *Camera Work*
1905	opens Little Galleries of the Photo-Secessionists at 291 Fifth Avenue
1915	publishes *291* magazine
1917	manages shows at the Anderson Galleries
1922	publishes *MSS* magazine
1925	opens The Intimate Gallery
1929	opens An American Place
JULY 13, 1946	Stieglitz dies of heart attack in New York City

Further Reading

Lowe, Sue Davidson. *Stieglitz: A Memoir/Biography.* New York: Farrar, Straus & Giroux, 1983. A comprehensive adult biography.

Naef, Weston J. *The Collection of Alfred Stieglitz.* New York: The Metropolitan Museum of Art, 1978. Complete information about the Stieglitz era with the photographs of his collection.

Norman, Dorothy. *Alfred Stieglitz: An American Seer.* Millerton, New York: Aperture Foundation, Inc., 1973. Quotations of Alfred Stieglitz by a woman who spent many years at his galleries; includes Stieglitz photographs.

Lewis W. Hine

(1874–1940)

At the turn of the 20th century, girls entered the cotton mills at the age of eight, and boys even younger. They were spinners, in charge of six or eight rows of rotating spools of cotton. When a thread broke, they tied it together. Lint covered them and filled their lungs, nose, ears, and eyes to the point of constant infection. They worked 10 to 15 hours a day, six days a week, every week, year after year until they died.

Lewis Hine wrote, "Let me tell you right here that these processes involve work, hard work, deadening in its monotony, exhausting physically, irregular, the workers' only joy the closing house. We might even say of these children that they are condemned to work."

For more than a decade, Hine took thousands of photographs that documented children at work so laws could be made to protect them.

Lewis W. Hine, *about 1925, photographer unknown. A champion of human rights, Hine took his camera to the docks, the mines, and the factories to depict the value of each person's life.* (Courtesy of Lewis W. Hine Collection, United States History, Local History and Genealogy Division, The New York Public Library, Astor, Lenox and Tilden Foundations)

The chairman of the National Child Labor Committee, Owen Lovejoy, said, "The work Hine did for the abolition of that evil was more responsible than all other efforts for bringing the facts and conditions of child employment to public attention."

The youngest of three children, Lewis Wickes Hine was born in Oshkosh, Wisconsin, on September 26, 1874. His father, Douglas Hull Hine, had been a drum major for the Union during the Civil War. His mother, Sarah Hayes Hine, had been a teacher before they moved to the Midwest. In Oshkosh the Hines operated a popular coffee shop and lived above the restaurant.

Just after Lewis graduated from high school, his father died in an accident. Lewis said, "My education was transferred for seven years to the manual side of factory, store, and bank. Here I lived behind the scenes in the life of the worker, gaining an understanding that increased through the years."

Lewis Hine worked 13 hours a day, six days a week, at an upholstery factory. After the factory was shut down, he delivered bundles for stores, sold water filters door-to-door, then took a job as a janitor in a bank. He studied stenography at night and became an assistant cashier. Later, he admitted he was "neither physically nor temperamentally fitted for any of these jobs."

Most likely he took night classes at the State Normal School. The principal of the school, Frank Manny, saw promise in Hine, offered him a part-time clerical job, and encouraged him to take education courses.

In 1900, Hine attended the University of Chicago for a year. Frank Manny, meanwhile, moved to New York as superintendent of the Ethical Culture School. Located in the city's Lower East Side, the progressive school offered courses in academics and the trades. Most of the pupils were emigrants from eastern Europe.

Manny offered Hine a position at the school teaching nature studies and geography. Hine moved to New York and immersed himself in the activities of students challenged by the new American culture. He also attended New York University, where he received a master of education degree in 1905.

Upon Manny's urging, Hine learned how to use a camera. He photographed students at school, in their workshops and classrooms, and he taught his students how the camera helped to see by focusing on details. Hine also published articles about the camera as a teaching aid. In the *Photographic Times,* he wrote, "The fundamental aim of the course is to help the pupils to better appreciation of good photography and how to attain it—in short, to give the artist's point of view, for, in the last analysis, good photography is a question of art."

"In the last analysis, good photography is a question of art."

Hine was excited about his camera work. All around him, he saw people and scenes he wanted to record. Millions of immigrants teemed into the city. They got off the huge steamers from Europe and were herded through facilities at Ellis Island. In 1904, Hine and Manny decided to photograph these individuals and families as they made their first wondrous steps in America.

Hine recalled how difficult the photographs were to get. Most of the immigrants did not speak English and certainly had never had their picture taken.

He said, "Now, suppose we are elbowing our way thro[ugh] the mob at Ellis trying to stop the surge of bewildered beings oozing through the corridors, up the stairs and all over the place, eager to get it all over and be on their way.

"Here is a small group that seems to have possibilities so we stop 'em and explain in pantomime that it would be lovely if they would only stick around just a moment. The rest of the human tide swirls around, often not too considerate of either the camera or us. We get the focus, on the ground glass, of course, then, hoping they will stay put, get the flash lamp ready."

Hine and Manny would prepare a flash gun, or a T-bar pan, with just the right mixture of magnesium, which was used as a flashpowder. Manny held the pan high while Hine went back to the camera. Manny ignited the chemical. It exploded, producing a blast of light, plumes of black smoke, and a loud bang, which led to the term *shooting* a picture.

Hine said, "It took all the resources of a hypnotist, a supersalesman, and a ball pitcher to prepare them to play the game and then to outguess them so most were not either wincing or shutting eyes when the time came to shoot."

Unfortunately for the immigrants, their first stop usually was the New York tenements, where they found work with people of their own culture. The buildings were filthy, with no electricity, no running water, and inadequate sanitation facilities. Families of a dozen or more members crowded into single rooms. When they

Mill Girl, *1908, by Lewis Hine. A 12-year-old mill worker's day might start at five o'clock in the morning and end 12 hours later, with only 10 minutes for lunch.*
(Library of Congress)

found work, they might bring it back to their rooms and engage the entire family—from the oldest grandparent to a two-year-old.

The immigrants also were met with anger and misunderstanding. Because they couldn't speak English, they were considered illiterate or stupid. Business operators offered them low wages, knowing they were desperate for work.

Hine saw the role that photography could play to document these people and their living conditions. Since the 1880s, photographs by writer and social reformer Jacob Riis had been published in newspapers and books to show the deplorable slums. But the public still generally felt that these people were lazy or inferior. Hine thought that photographs emphasizing their strength, enthusiasm, and determination might persuade people that being poor was just a social condition and that, with help, these people could rise above their situations.

Lewis Hine enrolled in graduate school at Columbia University, where he took classes at the School of Social Work. He met Paul Kellogg, the editor of a magazine, *Charities and the Commons* (later, *Survey* and *Graphic Survey*), which publicized the facts about child labor and tenement conditions. It was published by the National Child Labor Committee, one of many reform organizations that blossomed in the early decades of the 20th century. Created in 1904, the committee wanted to establish a minimum age of 14 for employment in manufacturing and 16 in mining, with no one under the age of 16 working more than eight hours a day or working at night.

The 1900 census reported that nearly 2 million children under the age of 16 were in the workforce. Children regularly were employed in factories, mines, and at home assembling clothing, artificial flowers, even picking nuts from their shells. They sold newspapers, worked as messengers, and took care of younger children. In the fields they picked and planted fruit, vegetables, and cotton, and at the docks they shelled shrimp and oysters.

Hine started accepting photo assignments for the National Child Labor Committee in 1906. He developed a style of having his subjects stare directly into the camera. Rather than evoking pity, he depicted pride and resolve of spirit.

During this time, in 1904, he had returned to Oshkosh to marry his sweetheart, Sara Ann Rich. They settled in Yonkers, New York, and had a son, Corydon. By 1908, Hine quit his teaching position and devoted all of his time to photography. He became a staff photographer for the National Child Labor Committee and for more than 15 years he traveled around the United States documenting child labor. In 1913 alone, he traveled 12,000 miles.

In the field, he was part of a three-person team. An investigator asked questions and wrote reports, a photographer took pictures, and a witness verified the truth of what was recorded and photographed. Hine worked in each capacity. His wife, Sara, often traveled with him as a witness.

In the *Child Labor Bulletin* of 1914, Hine wrote, "I have followed the procession of child workers winding through a thousand industrial communities, from the canneries of Maine to the fields of Texas. I have heard their tragic stories, watched their cramped lives and seen their fruitless struggles in the industrial game where the odds are all against them."

One subject Lewis Hine returned to again and again was the breaker boys. From the age of five, boys were sent into the coal mines. With their bare hands, breaker boys stooped over a chute and pulled out stones from the coal. They worked 12 to 14 hours a day. Like their counterparts in the mills, they suffered from lung and eye diseases. Some lost limbs or were crippled by machinery. Coal mining was dangerous, especially in the peak accident years of 1906 through 1910, when 84 coal mine disasters killed 2,494 miners, many of whom were children.

Factory and mine owners, of course, prevented investigators from entering their facilities. Hine would say he was a salesman or an industrial photographer making a record of machinery. If he couldn't get in, he waited outside. He asked the children their names and ages, how many hours they worked, and what they did. They also told him about their families and brothers and sisters.

Back in New York, Hine worked with Paul Kellogg, the magazine editor, to select photos, arrange page layouts, and write captions and articles. They used large headlines and made the photos prominent; sometimes captions were the only text. Hine called these layouts *photo*

Breaker Boys at a Pennsylvania Coal Mine, *1909, by Lewis Hine. Hine's photographs significantly influenced the public to make laws regulating child labor.* (Library of Congress)

stories. During his association with the committee, he had 189 photo stories published in the magazine, with the cover photo for 34 issues.

Hine also did freelance photography for other social welfare organizations, such as the National Consumers League. His photos were published in newspapers and such popular magazines as *McClure's* and *Everybody.* They also were printed in brochures and posters and displayed in exhibitions. He prepared slide shows and lectures and in 1914 became the exhibit director of the committee.

Hine called himself a "social photographer" and regularly advertised his services. When he wasn't traveling, he supervised the printing of his work, catalogued his extensive collection, and sent prints to photo agencies. Hine kept strict control over his negatives.

The stark Hine images and the exhaustive efforts of committee workers spread the word about child labor. Hine said, "I'm sure I am right in my choice of work. My child labor photos have already set the authorities to work to see if such things can be possible." Citizens pressured politicians to write legislation. From 1911 through 1913, 39 states passed child labor laws. A federal law was passed in 1916 but was repealed a few years later. Progress was made, but unfortunately many of the laws were not enforced.

World War I brought the Progressive Era to a close. Americans turned their attention to foreign soil and no longer responded to the reform movement at home. When the committee cut Hine's salary, he resigned.

In 1918, Hine was hired by the American Red Cross as a photographer, at the rank of captain. By this time, the war had been raging in Europe for four years. Known as the first modern war, World War I introduced gas warfare, heavy artillery, fighter planes, and bombs. Casualties were horrendous. Hine photographed Red Cross efforts helping the soldiers adjust to life away from home and providing medical rehabilitation. After the war ended, he was assigned to photograph some of the effects of the conflict. Typically, Hine focused his lens on children and refugees, depicting their courage and resolve.

"What a field for photographic art lies untouched in the industrial world. There is an urgent need for intelligent interpretation of the world's workers, not only for people of today, but for future ages."

"In Paris, after the armistice, I thought I had done my share of negative documentation," Hine later wrote. "I wanted to do something positive. So I said to myself, why not do the worker at work? The man on the job. At that time, he was as underprivileged as the kid in the mill."

For a long time, Hine had thought about a series depicting people at work. In his child labor studies he showed individuals overwhelmed by industrialization. Now he wanted to show that American workers were not dominated by machines; rather, it was their power and their skills that drove industry. He presented his vision to many organizations and foundations. As a result, he received assignments from the Amalgamated Clothing Workers Union, the National Tuberculosis Committee, the Tenement House Committee, the Boy Scouts and Girl Scouts, and the Interchurch World Movement.

In his work portraits, men and women build skyscrapers, manufacture steel, process food, etch glass, and run Linotype machines. They appear in their environment, engrossed in their work and proud of their participation in the new technologies. The photographs were published in several industry publications and were well received.

He labeled the back of the prints "men at work" or "women at work," then assembled a book, *Men at Work*, which was published in 1932. A book of his "women at work" photos was published after his death.

Hine asked public relations departments of companies to hire him to take photos of their factories. But few companies were prepared for Lewis Hine to enter their facilities with a camera. He did, however, receive assignments from such large companies as Western Electric and Shelton Looms, a progressive company that provided workers with insurance and a pension.

He also had a six-month commission to photograph construction of the Empire State Building in 1930. Assisted by his son, Corydon Hine, he took nearly 1,000 photographs of the tallest building in the world.

He recalled, "The day before, just before the high derrick was taken down, they swung me out in a box from the hundredth floor (a sheer drop of nearly a quarter of a mile) to get some shots of the tower. . . .

"I have always avoided dare-devil exploits and do not consider these experiences, with the cooperation the men have given me, as going quite that far, but they have given me a new zest of high adventure, and perhaps, a different note in my interpretation of industry."

The 1930s also brought Hine a number of commissions from government agencies. He photographed the construction of dams for the Tennessee Valley Authority and was a photographer for the National Research Project of the Works Projects Administration and the Rural Electrification Administration. But as time went on and the country fell into the Great Depression, he had more and more

Steamfitter, *1921, by Lewis Hine. "It is for the sake of emphasis, not exaggeration, that I select the more pictorial personalities when I do the industrial portrait," Hine said, "for it is only in this way that I can illustrate my thesis that the human spirit is the big thing after all."* (The Metropolitan Museum of Art, Ford Motor Company Collection, Gift of Ford Motor Company and John C. Waddell, 1987) (1987.1100.146)

difficulty earning a living. He received praise for his industrial photos, but the era of companies hiring photographers to show their businesses and factories was yet to come.

In the late 1930s, the bank repossessed Hine's house. Yet interest in his work had revived. With support from a number of photographers and sponsors, he had a one-man show at the Riverside Museum in New York City. He had exhibitions before, but this was his first retrospective. The museum displayed samples of all his work, from the child labor photos to the skyscrapers.

Hine was finally recognized as an artist. He was approached by television networks in New York and London to supply photographs to illustrate series of broadcasts on workers. He also was commissioned to prepare folios of his work for the Russell Sage Foundation. But he would not enjoy the surge of interest taken in his work. Late in 1939, his wife died. They had been married for 35 years, and he took it very hard. Lewis Hine himself fell ill the following year and died November 3, 1940, in Hastings-on-Hudson, New York.

Chronology

SEPTEMBER 26, 1874	Lewis Wickes Hine born in Oshkosh, Wisconsin
1892	works at several labor jobs
1900	works for State Normal School, Oshkosh; enrolls in University of Chicago
1901	moves to New York and teaches; enrolls in New York University
1905	receives master of education degree from New York University
1906	works as photographer for the National Child Labor Committee
1918	works as photographer for the American Red Cross in Europe
1919	begins work portrait series
1930	photographs construction of the Empire State Building
1932	publishes *Men at Work*
1933	works as photographer for federal agencies
1939	oversees retrospective one-man show at Riverside Museum
NOVEMBER 3, 1940	Hines dies in Hastings-on-Hudson, New York

Further Reading

Hine's Books
Hine, Lewis W. *Men at Work.* 1932. Reprint. New York: Dover Publications and the International Museum of Photography at George Eastman House, 1977. Hine's photographs of workers.
Hine, Lewis W. *Women at Work.* New York: Dover Publications and the International Museum of Photography at George Eastman House, 1981. Hine's photographs with introductory text.

Books About Lewis W. Hine
Freedman, Russell. *Kids At Work: Lewis Hine and the Crusade Against Child Labor.* New York: Clarion Books, 1994. Illustrated, easy-to-read young adult biography.
Trachtenberg, Alan. *America and Lewis Hine.* Millerton, New York: Aperture, Inc., 1977. Comprehensive adult biography, illustrated.

Edward Steichen

(1879–1973)

In 1903, Edward Steichen was asked to photograph the great financier J. Pierpont Morgan, one of the most powerful men in the world. Morgan had commissioned a German artist, Fedor Encke, to paint his portrait, but he was too restless to pose for it. Encke asked Steichen to take a photograph that he could use as a guide.

Steichen arrived early. He asked the building janitor to pose in Morgan's place so he could set up his equipment.

"Morgan arrived with Encke," Steichen later wrote, "took off his large hat, laid a foot-long cigar on the edge of the table, sat in the chair previously occupied by the janitor, and took his habitual Encke portrait pose."

Self-Portrait with Palette, 1901, by Edward Steichen. The young Steichen became a master at the gum bichromate process, which made photographs look like paintings. (Collection of the J. Paul Getty Museum, Malibu, California. Reprinted with permission of Joanna T. Steichen.)

Steichen made a two- or three-second exposure on a glass plate in his camera. Then he suggested that Morgan move his hands and head to a different position.

"He took the head position," Steichen added, "but said, in an irritated tone, that it was uncomfortable, so I suggested he move his head to a position that felt natural.

"He moved his head several times and ended exactly where it had been 'uncomfortable' before, except that this time he took the pose of his own volition. But his expression had sharpened and his body posture became tense, possibly a reflex of his irritation at the suggestion I had made. I saw that a dynamic self-assertion had taken place, whatever its cause, and I quickly made the second exposure, saying, 'Thank you, Mr. Morgan,' and I took the plate holder out of the camera.

"He said, 'Is that all?'

"'Yes, sir,' I answered.

"He snorted a reply. 'I like you, young man. I think we'll get along first-rate together.' Then he clapped his large hat on his massive head, took up his big cigar, and stormed out of the room. Total time three minutes."

For the young photographer, looking Morgan in the eye had been "like confronting the headlights of an express train."

☆ ☆ ☆

Edouard (later, Edward) Jean Steichen was born March 27, 1879, in Luxembourg. His parents came from peasant families and immigrated to the United States to provide more opportunity for their son. His father, Jean-Pierre Steichen, and mother, Marie Kemp Steichen, settled in Hancock, Michigan, where his sister, Lillian, was born.

Edward's father worked in copper mines until his health failed, then in 1889 the family moved to Milwaukee, Wisconsin. There, his mother supported the family with a millinery shop where she designed, decorated, and sold hats.

At an early age, Edward showed artistic promise but his mother could not afford to send him to art school. When he was 15, he accepted a four-year apprenticeship at the American Fine Art Gallery, a shop that created lithographs, posters, and other printed materials for advertising and public relations.

To enhance his skills in drawing and painting, Edward organized a group of students into the Milwaukee Art Students' League. They hired models to pose and asked professional artists to critique their work. Edward created a noteworthy portfolio of watercolors, oil paintings, and drawings. As an illustrator and graphic designer, he became good enough to be hired by the shop after his apprenticeship and won an award for envelope design.

"*Emotional reaction to the qualities of places, things, and people became the principal goal in my photography.*"

Influenced by the growing popularity of photography, at the age of 16 Edward bought a secondhand camera that held a roll of 50 negatives. Only one photo came from that first roll, but he already had grown to love the process of taking photographs. He particularly enjoyed going out in late afternoons to photograph the woods in drizzly rain or snow, or taking pictures of his friends in the dappled sunshine. Like many amateur photographers of the day, he tried to imitate paintings. He joggled the tripod or put water on the lens to get an impressionistic feeling.

Steichen also saw the commercial advantages of photography. With a partner, he operated a photography business in his spare time. They took pictures of social outings, clubs, and portraits for 25 to 50 cents each.

At the American Fine Art Gallery, he complained that the company's illustrations were too old-fashioned. He later wrote, "The firm did a good deal of work for brewers, flour mills, and pork packers. Neither the pigs nor the wheat shown in our library of old woodcuts looked anything like those I had seen at the Wisconsin State Fair, or during my summer vacations in the country. So I suggested to the manager of the design department that we make photographs."

His manager agreed and Steichen traded in his small camera and bought a large view camera that took glass negatives. He converted his basement into a darkroom and spent hours experimenting with chemical processes. Outdoors, he photographed his favorite scenes over and over at different times of day to determine how light affects photographs.

Very little was published about photography in the late 1890s, but Steichen read what he could find; he studied *Camera Notes*, the publication of the New York Camera Club edited by Alfred Stieglitz.

Rodin—Le Penseur, *1902, by Edward Steichen. Long an admirer of the sculptor Auguste Rodin, Steichen combined two negatives to create the image of the artist contemplating two of his works*—Victor Hugo *and* The Thinker. (Collection of the J. Paul Getty Museum, Malibu, California. Reprinted with permission of Joanna T. Steichen.)

He also read a magazine article about the Philadelphia Photographic Salon of 1898, one of the first exhibitions of photographs in America. The next year he entered his photos, and three were exhibited in the Second Philadelphia Photographic Salon. Three photos were also accepted at the Chicago Salon. At the age of 20, Edward Steichen had achieved significant recognition for the quality of his photography.

After two years of full-time work at the lithography shop, Steichen was ready to start his career in Paris, the city known as a center for trend-setting artists. Along the way he stopped in New York. To his delight, he saw one of his advertising designs covering a six-story warehouse.

Steichen visited Alfred Stieglitz at the New York Camera Club. Stieglitz already had earned a reputation as an excellent photographer who promoted photography as art. Carefully looking at each piece of art in Steichen's portfolio, Stieglitz was very impressed with the young painter-photographer. He even bought three photographs.

As Steichen left, Alfred Stieglitz said, "Well I suppose now that you're going to Paris, you'll forget about photography and devote yourself entirely to painting."

Steichen replied, "I will always stick to photography!"

After renting a studio in Paris, Steichen energetically pursued both painting and photography. In 1901 more than 20 of his photographs were shown at an exhibition called "The New School of American Photography," in London and in Paris. One of his paintings was shown at the prestigious National Salon of Fine Arts. He even had a one-man show of paintings and photographs, which he called "painting with light."

Steichen became a master at a type of photographic manipulation called *gum bichromate*. Using a variety of chemicals, he would coat light-sensitive paper with a brush to make a granular effect. He would cover the paper with the glass negative and expose them to sunlight or ultraviolet light. Not all of the chemicals would dry and he could brush the surface again while he washed it in water to get a photograph that looked like a painting. Steichen also was one of the first to experiment with color photography.

Within two years, Steichen returned to the United States. He settled in New York City and rented upstairs space at 291 Fifth Avenue, the same building where Stieglitz had his gallery. He put up a small showcase on the street level to advertise his work, and he hung out a shingle as a professional portrait photographer. People passing by would see his showcase and make an appointment to have their portraits taken. Satisfied clients referred their friends, and soon his business blossomed. Steichen was a good businessman who commanded high fees. Personable and handsome, he was six feet tall and had learned how to charm wealthy patrons. He was known for his sense of humor and the interest he took in children.

About the same time Steichen established his New York studio, Alfred Stieglitz split from the New York Camera Club and produced his exhibition, "American Pictorial Photography Arranged by the Photo-Secession." Fourteen of Steichen's photographs were included, and Steichen was praised as one of the finest photographers in the exhibition.

Steichen designed the cover, layout, and type for Stieglitz's new publication, *Camera Work*. He also became Stieglitz's favorite photographer. During the 15 years of the magazine's publication, 71 of Steichen's photographs were reproduced and three issues were entirely devoted to him. Steichen's photographs also were prominent in American and European exhibitions, where he won many prizes.

In 1903 Edward Steichen married Clara E. Smith, whom he had met in Paris. They spent their honeymoon at the Stieglitz estate at Lake George and would have two daughters, Mary and Kate.

Edward Steichen still was entranced with Europe and moved back in 1906. He settled his family in a farmhouse at Voulangis, about 30 miles from Paris. There, he developed a passion for raising delphiniums, beautiful flowers that grow in tall, five-foot spikes covered with blossoms. He also learned how to pilot an airplane. In the French countryside, he concentrated on painting while he did some photographic portraits and fashion photography. He and his family lived simply.

Steichen often went to museums and art exhibitions and especially enjoyed meeting artists and writers. He took photos of the artists Auguste Rodin and Henri Matisse, the writer George Bernard Shaw, and the dancer Isadora Duncan. Many prominent up-and-coming artists were in his social circle, and he convinced Stieglitz to show their work in his gallery in New York. These artists—including Paul Cézanne, Édouard Manet, Pablo Picasso, and Henri Toulouse-Lautrec—became some of the most influential and famous of all modern artists.

Steichen also spent time in the United States. His photograph of J. Pierpont Morgan and recognition from exhibitions helped build his reputation. He received commissions to photograph U.S. presidents Theodore Roosevelt and William Howard Taft. When his sister Lillian married the poet Carl Sandburg in 1908, Sandburg and Steichen became fast friends and remained close the rest of their lives.

As Europe clashed forces at the start of World War I in 1914, Steichen and his family left their French farmhouse just two days before the German army camped out in their yard. Steichen volunteered for the United States Army after the Americans entered the war in 1917.

He said, "I wanted to be a photographic reporter, as Mathew Brady had been in the Civil War, and I went to Washington to offer my services, with the endorsement of the Camera Clubs of America."

He became the commander of the photographic division, and, like Brady, created darkrooms on the battlefields. Many of the photographers worked out of trucks with electricity powered by generators. Rather than the soft painterly images of pictorial photography, war images, and especially aviation photography, required sharp detail. Steichen would use this technique in his photography from then on.

With the rank of army colonel, Steichen returned to his house in Voulangis after the war, replanted his delphiniums, and resumed painting interiors and flowers.

One morning he walked into his art studio and discovered a flower painting on his palette. He called to the gardener, who admitted he had created the painting. Steichen said it was better

"*I wanted to reach into the world, to participate and communicate, and I felt I would be able to do this best through photography.*"

J. Pierpont Morgan, *1903, by Edward Steichen. When Steichen asked Morgan to move, he responded with a powerful expression of anger. From that experience, Steichen said, "The essential thing was to awaken a genuine response."* (The Metropolitan Museum of Art, The Alfred Stieglitz Collection, 1949. Reprinted with permission of Joanna T. Steichen.)

than what he had been trying to do. He threw all of the paintings into the yard and burned them in a bonfire. From then on, Steichen was through with painting. "Photography was to be my medium," he later wrote. "I wanted to reach into the world, to participate and communicate, and I felt I would be able to do this best through photography."

As he had when he first began photography, Edward Steichen threw himself into experimentation. He took more than a thousand photographs of a white cup and saucer placed on a scale of gray tones from pure white to black velvet. He analyzed and photographed such natural formations as the spiral and took close-up pictures that created abstract forms.

By the early 1920s, Steichen decided to return to New York and commit himself to the profession of photography. When he got to New York, he bought a copy of *Vanity Fair*. His picture was in the magazine with the caption, "The greatest living portrait photographer." It said he had unfortunately given up photography.

Steichen wrote a letter to the editor, thanked him for the tribute and corrected him that he had given up painting, not photography. He was offered a job as chief photographer of Condé Nast Publications, publishers of *Vanity Fair* and numerous other magazines. A few days later, when asked, he stated what he thought he should be paid. The publisher said it was more than they had ever paid any photographer.

Steichen answered, "It was not *my* statement published in *Vanity Fair* that I was the greatest living portrait photographer."

Edward Steichen became the highest paid photographer in the world. His large studio was a converted carriage house from the days before cars. He would drive up in his yellow convertible roadster and ring the bell for someone to open the doors, then he would drive into the studio and park next to the receptionist's desk. Along with assignments for magazines, he did photographs for advertising accounts.

Of that period Steichen said, "Many people were bothering me to do portraits of them. So, as a way of stalling them off, I said I would have to charge a thousand a picture. When that got around, more people came for portraits than ever before."

He photographed people of great importance, from world leaders such as President Franklin Delano Roosevelt and Prime Minister Winston Churchill, to novelist Willa Cather and composer George Gershwin. He also took many photographs of such Hollywood stars as Greta Garbo, Charlie Chaplin, Paul Robeson, and Fred Astaire.

Actress Lillian Gish said, "He liked the human race and he showed you the human race as you'd take pictures of flowers—at their best, most handsome, and most beautiful."

Even though he was the most revered photographer of his time, Steichen continued to experiment. Like all photographers of the early twentieth century, he had relied on natural light. Both as a teenager and in his French garden, Steichen had studied the effects of sun on subjects he photographed. In his New York studio, he studied how electric light illuminated objects and affected negatives. He hung lights on stands and on bars across the ceiling at all angles to create dramatic images of light and shadow. He used large white boards or umbrellas to deflect the light and make people's faces look softer. Steichen also was one of the first commercial photographers to photograph models with horses or pianos, dressed in all white or all black, or in the throes of high drama.

In his autobiography, *A Life in Photography,* Steichen wrote, "When an artist of any kind looks at his subject, he looks with everything he is. Everything that he has lived, learned, observed, and experienced combines to enable him to identify himself with the subject and look with insight, perception, imagination, and understanding."

In his personal life, Steichen's marriage of 20 years had ended in divorce, and in 1923 he married Dana Desboro Glover, a model. They bought a 425-acre farm in Redding, Connecticut, in 1929, and Steichen built a 25-acre pond. He continued his passion of growing delphiniums and at one point had about 50,000 plants. His delphiniums were so magnificent that the Museum of Modern Art exhibited them.

In 1938, Steichen decided to close his studio. Fashion photography had become too routine, and he disliked some of the advertising approaches. "Among these were the sex appeal approaches designed to sell lotions or cosmetics or hair preparations by implying that a

The Flatiron—Evening, *1904, by Edward Steichen. Pictured in the mist, New York's triangular Flatiron Building was a symbol of the new, modern age.* (The Metropolitan Museum of Art, Alfred Stieglitz Collection, 1933. Reprinted with permission of Joanna T. Steichen)

girl stood no chance of finding a mate unless she used these products. But the real fault was my own. I had lost interest because I no longer found the work challenging; it was too easy."

When the United States entered World War II, Edward Steichen volunteered. Although he was 62 years old, he became the commander of navy combat photography and received the rank of navy captain. During his four years of service, he arranged two exhibitions of photographs depicting military power, at the Museum of Modern Art. He also supervised photography for the 1944 war movie *The Fighting Lady.*

After the war, Steichen was appointed the director of the department of photography at the Museum of Modern Art and started a new career. For 15 years he added to the museum's permanent collection and arranged 44 shows. His most ambitious exhibition of photographs was called "The Family of Man."

In the book that reproduced the photos of the exhibition, he wrote, "It was conceived as a mirror of the universal elements and emotions in the everydayness of life—as a mirror of the essential oneness of mankind throughout the world."

Steichen sent requests all over the world and received submissions of about 2 million photographs. These were culled to 10,000 prints, and finally to 503 photos from 68 countries, representing 273 photographers. "The Family of Man" opened in 1955 and broke all attendance records. The show toured 37 countries and was seen in person by 9 million people.

"I finally came to the conclusion that the deep interest in this show was based on a kind of audience participation." He added, "the people in the audience looked at the pictures, and the people in the pictures looked back at them. They recognized each other."

While the exhibition was touring the world, Steichen's wife, Dana, died. He was deeply saddened and his health worsened. When he went to the opening of "The Family of Man" in Russia, he met the woman who would be his third wife, Joanna Traub.

For his work and his contributions to the art of photography, Steichen received many honorary degrees and awards from organizations of artists, photographers, architects, and botanists. His photographs were shown in one-man exhibitions, and museums purchased Steichen prints for their collections.

President John F. Kennedy awarded Steichen the Presidential Medal of Freedom in 1963. After Kennedy's untimely death, Steichen received the award from President Lyndon B. Johnson, who said, "Photographer and collector, he has made the camera the instrument of perception and thereby transformed a science into an art."

In his retirement, Steichen enjoyed his Connecticut estate and conducted yet another photographic experiment. In all kinds of light, at all seasons, and in all types of weather, he took photographs and filmed a beautiful shadblow tree at the edge of his pond, always examining the enticing play of light and shadow, sun and shade.

Edward Steichen died in Redding, Connecticut, March 25, 1973, at the age of 93.

Chronology

MARCH 27, 1879	Edward Jean Steichen born in Luxembourg
1894	works for American Fine Art Gallery
1897	organizes Milwaukee Art Students' League
1899	has his photos shown at Second Philadelphia Photographic Salon
1900	moves to Paris and begins to exhibit paintings and photographs
1902	moves to New York City and opens photo studio
1903	marries Clara E. Smith
1906	returns to France and concentrates on painting
1914	returns to New York
1917	volunteers for U.S. Army, becomes commander of photographic division
1923	works as chief photographer for *Vogue* and *Vanity Fair*; begins advertising photography; marries Dana Desboro Glover
1942	becomes commander of navy combat photography
1947	appointed director of department of photography, Museum of Modern Art
1955	organizes "The Family of Man" exhibit
1960	marries Joanna Traub
1963	receives Presidential Medal of Freedom from President Lyndon B. Johnson
MARCH 25, 1973	Steichen dies in Redding, Connecticut

Further Reading

Steichen's Books
Steichen, Edward. *A Life in Photography*. Garden City, New York: Doubleday and Company in collaboration with the Museum of Modern Art, 1963. Steichen's first-person account of his life and career, fully illustrated.

Books About Edward Steichen
Introduction by Ruth Kelton. *Edward Steichen*. Millerton, New York: Aperture, Inc., 1978. Steichen photographs with short introduction.
Sandburg, Carl, Alexander Liberman, Edward Steichen, and Rene d'Harnoncourt. *Steichen the Photographer*. New York: The Museum of Modern Art, 1961. Steichen photographs with essay by Carl Sandburg.

Video About Edward Steichen
Zimmerman, Christopher, producer and director, written by Lou Buttino. *A Century in Photography*. Public Broadcasting System, 1980. From a television presentation, with commentary and Steichen photographs.

Dorothea Lange

(1895–1966)

One day in March 1936, Dorothea Lange was on her way home, back from a hard trip. Thoughts of her family and a warm house beckoned her. But she still had over 450 miles to go. It would be a long drive in the rain.

Out of the corner of her eye, she saw a sign for a pea-pickers' camp. She convinced herself to keep on driving, five miles, 10 miles, 20 miles past. Then abruptly she made a U-turn and returned to that sign on the road.

No one was picking that day. She entered the camp and went directly to a makeshift shelter.

Dorothea recalled, "I saw and approached the hungry and desperate mother, as if drawn by a magnet. I do not remember how I explained my presence or my camera to her, but I do remember she asked me no questions. . . . She told me her age, that she was 32. She

Dorothea Lange, 1936, by Rondal Partridge. Lange and several other photographers were paid by the federal government to take images of Americans during the Great Depression. (© 1995 Rondal Partridge)

said that they had been living on frozen vegetables from the surrounding fields and the birds that the children killed. She had just sold the tires from her car to buy food. There she sat in that lean-to tent with her children huddled around her and seemed to know that my pictures might help her, and so she helped me. There was a sort of equality about it."

Dorothea took five photographs of the woman and her children. As soon as she got back to her darkroom, she developed the film. Immediately she delivered prints to the San Francisco *News,* which carried the story of the stranded workers. Other newspapers also printed the story. As a result, 20,000 pounds of food from the federal government were delivered to the starving families.

Dorothea Margaretta Nutzhorn was born on May 25, 1895, and grew up in Hoboken, New Jersey. She had a bout with polio when she was seven that left her right leg permanently affected so she could not flex her foot. She was ashamed of her limp and throughout her life recognized how it shaped her personality.

Her father, Henry Nutzhorn, abandoned the family when Dorothea was 12. She and her younger brother, Martin, were brought up by her mother, Joanna Lange, and her German grandmother, Sophie.

At that time, Joanna Lange worked at the public library on the Lower East Side of Manhattan. She enrolled Dorothea in a public school in that neighborhood so they could commute together. After school, Dorothea wandered the streets. She would eventually wind up at the library reading room, where she enjoyed looking at books with pictures.

After high school, Dorothea enrolled in the New York Training School for Teachers because her family wanted her to. She wasn't interested in a teaching career—one of the few open to women at that time—since she never had been a good student. She was more fascinated by the visual arts, such as advertising posters and pictures in photographers' studio windows. Even though she had never taken a photograph, Dorothea was convinced she could earn a living at photography and told her mother she wanted to be a photographer.

So she could get all kinds of photography experience, Dorothea took jobs with a series of New York photographers. Her first was working for Arnold Genthe, a famous portrait photographer with an exclusive clientele. Genthe had lived in San Francisco, where he documented life in Chinatown before the 1906 fire.

At his studio, Dorothea learned how to pose clients and put them at ease while their photos were taken. She worked in the darkroom where she learned how to retouch photographs to make people look better. She used India ink to fix light areas on negatives, a process called spotting. Dorothea also made prints and mounted finished photographs.

At another studio, she worked for a woman who hired photographers. When her camera operator didn't show up one day, out of desperation the woman sent Dorothea. The client was very satisfied with her work, and Dorothea became one of the studio's principal photographers.

She quit school and took a photography course at Columbia University from Clarence White, a prominent photographer of Alfred Stieglitz's group known as the Photo-Secessionists. Dorothea was influenced by White's soft-focus, luminous photographs.

When Dorothea was 23, she announced that she and her long-time friend, Florence (Fronsie) Ahlstrom, were planning to make their way around the world. Fronsie worked at Western Union, which had many branches. Dorothea had her camera. They traveled as far as San Francisco. The first morning out, however, their money was stolen. So the next day they each got jobs. Fronsie, of course, slipped into a position at Western Union. Dorothea took a counter position at the Marsh Photo-Supply House. She also formally took her mother's last name, Lange.

Within a few months, a businessman set Lange up in her own photography studio. She leased half a building and the basement of 540 Sutter Street, which stood behind an art gallery that sold etchings and fine prints.

Like the owners of the studios where she had worked in New York, Dorothea Lange established a commercial portrait studio. Her business flourished. She used a heavy, large-format 8 x 10 camera and did all the developing and printing in her basement darkroom. Finished prints were mounted on handmade Japanese paper with a scalloped edge called *deckle.*

The large studio became a meeting place for various friends, many of whom were artists. Lange kept a big samovar that her assistant lit every afternoon to serve visitors tea, and she had a black velvet couch that was famous for sparking proposals of marriage. In the evenings, the rug would be rolled back so her friends could dance to a phonograph.

That was where she met lean, weathered Maynard Dixon. He was an illustrator and mural painter 20 years older than Lange. Six months later they were married. They were a spectacular couple. Dixon wore an elegant wide-brimmed hat and a cape. Lange also wore a cape and a beret. People would turn and look at them when they entered a room.

Maynard Dixon had earned a prominent reputation for his paintings of western themes. A native Californian born in 1875, he especially liked to render images of cattlemen on the open range or friends in the Hopi and Navajo nations. He often went away on painting and sketching expeditions. These separations made Lange's young married life difficult. Dixon's 10-year-old daughter lived with them, and they had two sons of their own, born three years apart. Lange struggled to manage a household and a thriving business at the same time.

The stock market crash of 1929 drastically cut into her business. Clients didn't have the extra money to have their photos taken. Her husband's art sales were even more seriously affected, and the family income dropped. To make matters worse, the marriage was dissolving. Lange and Dixon each moved into their own studio, though they continued to see each other. Reluctantly, Lange sent her sons to boarding school.

The next few years dramatically affected the American economy. Across the country, farmers were in a slump. Markets to sell produce had fallen since the government had stopped famine relief to other countries in 1922. Intensive single-crop farming depleted soil re-

Migrant Mother, *1936, by Dorothea Lange. One of the most famous photographs of all time,* Migrant Mother *is a symbol of endurance. Protecting her children, the woman draws on great inner strength while she gazes into the horizon.* (Library of Congress)

sources. Several years of particularly dry weather also had affected crops.

In 1933, the Agricultural Adjustment Act was signed into law. It paid farmers to allow land to lie fallow, or unused. The act was designed as a relief. Landowners who had survived the decade bought tractors with the relief money. Those who couldn't make payments on borrowed money became tenant farmers. With all the unused land, tenant farmers became day laborers. Thousands of farm families were forced off the land. They were "tractored out."

In the mid-1930s, the great black blizzards—dust storms—raged across the plains. They ripped up the unplanted land, which was very dry because of the drought. Such states as Oklahoma, Texas, and Arkansas became known as Dust Bowl states. With no signs of work, no land to grow food, and landowners threatening them at gunpoint, families moved west. They had heard about abundant sunshine, fruit trees—and jobs.

"The first wave of those people arrived in Southern California on a weekend," Lange remembered. "It was as sharp and sudden as that when I was there. . . . A month later they were trying to close the border."

Because there were too many workers, business owners exploited them with long hours and no guarantees of work. People who picked fruit and vegetables would only be hired until the work was done, then had to move on. Underpaid dock workers performed grueling tasks for up to 36 hours straight. Then they often had to wait weeks for more work.

Under the direction of strong leaders, more than 12,000 dock workers organized one of the most crippling strikes in history. In the July 1934 maritime strike, demonstrators fought in the streets with business managers. Spectators were wounded and two men were killed. But the strikers won.

Lange and Dixon were drawn to the crowds at the docks. Dixon sketched and Lange photographed the scenes. She said, "I was just gathering my forces and that took a little bit because I wasn't accustomed to jostling about in groups of tormented, depressed and angry men with a camera."

One of her friends, photographer Willard Van Dyke, was impressed with Lange's new direction in photography. In *Camera Craft*, he published a biography of Dorothea Lange that was illustrated with five of her photographs. He also hung an exhibition of her prints at his Oakland gallery.

There, Paul Taylor first saw Lange's work. Taylor was a professor of economics at the University of California, Berkeley. He used Lange's photos to illustrate articles he wrote. When he became the field director for the newly formed State Emergency Relief Administration, he knew he needed photographs and hired Lange.

Lange's first assignments were in the California valleys. There, she witnessed the extreme conditions migrant farm workers were living under. They had no sanitation and scant water supplies. They lived in lean-tos and shelters made from scraps of wood or metal. Some came on foot. Others had arrived in jalopies—old, run-down cars— and trucks. The promises of a golden California fell tragically short;

Plantation Overseer and Field Hands, *1936, by Dorothea Lange. Social order can clearly be shown by facial expressions and how people sit or stand.* (Library of Congress)

DOROTHEA LANGE

there were far too many eager hands for available work, and the average pay was only 27 cents an hour. "Company" stores stocked provisions because the workers had no transportation into local towns. But they charged high prices, forcing workers into debt.

Typhoid, smallpox, and tuberculosis killed the undernourished. The ill and injured were rejected at the hospital doors. Medical treatment would be at state expense, and they weren't state residents. Even burial fees ran high, so families buried their dead in unmarked graves along the side of a road or in a field.

The first Taylor-Lange report of 1935 was illustrated with 57 photos depicting squalid living conditions. Paul Taylor recommended that the state ask for federal funds to build camps for migratory laborers. The Federal Emergency Relief Administration came through with $20,000. Camps were built in the Imperial and San Joaquin valleys. They featured buildings for community use, an office for the camp manager, and raised platforms for tents. There were toilet and shower facilities, fresh water, and stoves. But they housed only a limited number of people and many more were needed.

"Their roots were all torn out," Dorothea Lange said. "I had to get my camera to register the things about those people that were more important than how poor they were—their pride, their strength, their spirit."

The Taylor group was not alone in its efforts to house and retrain the migrants. In April 1935, President Roosevelt's executive order created the Resettlement Administration (RA). It was under the direction of the U.S. Department of Agriculture. The purpose was to provide loans to poor farmers and develop conservation projects to stop soil erosion. Thousands of homeless Americans would also be resettled.

Roy Stryker, an assistant professor of economics at Columbia, was hired as director of the historical section of the Farm Security Administration (FSA). He supplied information to magazines, syndicates, films and radio programs, and maintained a file of photographs. Dorothea Lange was hired as a photographer-investigator.

At the age of 40, Dorothea Lange was at last thoroughly engaged in the work she found most fulfilling. She closed her portrait studio.

Her sons continued to attend boarding school so she could spend time on her work, but she hated being separated from them.

After 15 years of marriage, her husband Maynard went to Nevada for a divorce. But they kept an amiable relationship for the rest of their lives. Dorothea turned to Paul Taylor. He was a sturdy, consistent man committed to the same cause that she was. They worked in partnership and a romance developed; they married in New Mexico in 1936. Unfortunately, their deep involvement with field work meant their children had to be kept in foster homes.

The migrants were suspicious of government workers entering the camps. So Lange developed her own methods to earn their trust. She would ask for a cup of water, and take a long time drinking it. "My acceptance, finally, of my lameness, truly opened gates for me," she admitted. "When I was working with people who were strangers to me, where I walk into situations where I am very much an outsider, to be a crippled person, or a disabled person, gives an immense advantage. People are kinder to you. It puts you on a different level than if you go into a situation whole and secure. . . ."

Lange's particular style was emerging through her field work in photography. She communicated so much presence in a photograph of a man's back or hands clenched on a hoe. Her focus was on the small gesture—a palm against a worried brow, a foot drawing circles in the dirt, or a protective embrace of a mother promising her child that tomorrow will be better.

In 1937 and 1938, Lange and Taylor made several trips around the country to meet the people who hadn't migrated. Their journey across 17,000 miles of the American landscape exposed them to the poverty of more than nine million people. They went to the fields to record day laborers haying, hauling, and raking. The workers picked such crops as corn, cotton, peas, oats, and peaches for 75 cents a day. Lange and Taylor also visited turpentine camps, mining towns, and garment factories.

" I *realize more and more what it takes to be a really good photographer. You go in over your head, not just up to your neck.* "

Not all of her subjects were the destitute. Dorothea Lange took photos of children and teenagers playing music, smiling, laughing. In one photo she pictured the women of a small town at the steps of their church on town cleaning day. Lange would take several shots, moving in closer each time until she had a tight composition of a stance or a face.

Roy Stryker was pleased with the work from all his photographers. Resettlement Administration photos were on public display in schools, churches, town councils, and clubs, and Stryker especially received calls for Lange's pictures. More newspapers, press services, and magazines were picking up the stories of the drought and migration. Editorials supported creating more camps.

Lange prepared photographs for the rush of requests she received. The College Art Association financed a traveling exhibit of 110 RA photographs. The San Francisco Museum of Art and Mills College also created exhibitions about the 1930s. She eagerly captioned her photos with the notes she jotted down when she took the shots.

In October 1936, the writer John Steinbeck used Lange's photos to illustrate a series of articles for the San Francisco *News*. Steinbeck was a strong advocate of the rights of migratory workers and learned about their lives from Lange. Earlier that year, he had published *In Dubious Battle*, a novel about fruit pickers trying to organize and fight the injustices of growers. Later, he would publish *Grapes of Wrath*, the dramatic story of a migrant family. When director John Ford made the book into a movie, he used Lange's photographs to establish the look of the film.

Through the years, many critics had tried to define the type of photography that Lange did. It stressed emotional impact while directly recording actual events. Stryker called it "pictorial document." Others called it *documentary photography*, the name that stuck. For Lange, documentary photography was not a question of subject matter but of approach. She said that the important thing is not what's photographed, but how.

By the end of this era, Roy Stryker and his staff of 11 photographers had authorized, taken, and organized more than 270,000 photographs. The character of America's people and their relationship to a changing economy was captured for all time.

Japanese Onlookers, *1942, by Dorothea Lange. Japanese-Americans were taken from their homes and placed in camps during World War II out of fear they would side with Japan rather than the United States.* (National Archives)

After her FSA work ended in 1939, Lange took the opportunity to stay home more than she had in years. Lange and Taylor had a loving, solid marriage. When they could, they brought their children home to a stable environment. They bought a house in Berkeley where she had a darkroom and a studio built.

In 1941, Lange received a financial grant from the Guggenheim Foundation. She was the first woman and only the third photographer to receive the prestigious grant. She photographed cooperative communities in South Dakota, Iowa, and Utah. She continued to travel and photograph but began to be more and more bothered by stomach pains and an ulcer.

DOROTHEA LANGE

In December 1941, the Japanese military bombed Pearl Harbor, a U.S. naval base in Hawaii. A type of hysteria arose against Japanese immigrants and Americans of Japanese descent. Americans feared that these people, most of whom lived along the California coast, would somehow aid the enemy. Japanese-Americans, however, wanted to prove their loyalty to the United States. Many young men joined the armed services and became some of the most decorated soldiers in the war.

The United States government made Japanese-Americans move from their homes into camps built in the Owens Valley in California. Like many Americans, Lange was horrified. She was hired by the Office of War Information to document the camps. She started by photographing in the Japanese neighborhoods of San Francisco, where the decrees were posted and the people were rounded up for relocation. She sympathized with their bewilderment and admired their courage.

Very few of these photos were publicized at the time. Late in 1944, the United States Supreme Court ruled that loyal citizens could not be held in detention camps against their will, and inmates were permitted to leave. It was not until 1988 that the government truly acknowledged its mistake, apologized officially, and paid these people money for their hardship.

"Artists are controlled by the life that beats in them, like the ocean beats on the shore. They are almost pursued; there's something constantly acting upon them from the outside world that shapes their existence."

During the war years she also was hired by the Office of War Information to illustrate the American spirit. On assignments with no assistant, she lugged her cameras around to Italian, Yugoslavian, and Hispanic communities to document minorities on the West Coast. Many of these pictures were used for overseas publications.

Lange was hospitalized several times, underwent surgery, and was extremely ill, too sick to work for several years. As she regained her health, she participated in conferences. Her work was shown regularly in major gallery exhibitions and museums. From time to time, she accepted short assignments for such magazines as *Look* and *Life,* including a photo essay about Ireland.

Although she kept working, Lange was so ill that she often slept half sitting up. Mostly because of her illness, but also because she felt she had never been part of a close family either as a child or as a mother, she now wanted to focus on her family. Through the summer months she and her husband took their grandchildren to a rented cabin at Stinson Beach in Northern California. She became the matriarchal grandmother who voiced her sympathy or enthusiasm to every member of the family. At holidays, she orchestrated festivities and during the year she wrote notes to those who didn't live nearby.

She traveled with her husband to Japan, Korea, Indonesia, India, Russia, and Europe—finally completing the round-the-world trip she had started in her youth. She also traveled to South America and Egypt. Although she was frustrated that she couldn't recreate the in-depth photo essays of her younger years, she did take thousands of exposures.

Back home, she taught, worked on book projects of her photographs, and allowed documentary films to be made about her. Then in 1964 she was diagnosed with cancer.

The same determination that had guided her in her career, however, drove her to complete one more major project. The Museum of Modern Art in New York wanted a show of her works, a great honor for any artist, and the first time they had asked a woman photographer. In earnest, she went through thousands of negatives to form the exhibit—a lifetime of photographs. After more than a year of preparing the show, mostly in great pain, she was finally satisfied with the themes and the presentation of her work.

In October 1965, she was hospitalized for the last time and died at the age of 70. The well-attended "Dorothea Lange Retrospective" opened five months later.

Chronology

MAY 25, 1895	Dorothea Margaretta Nutzhorn born in Hoboken, New Jersey
1918	moves to San Francisco and opens portrait studio
1920	marries Maynard Dixon
1934	begins photographing people of the Depression
1935	closes studio; marries Paul Taylor
1935	works for Resettlement Administration, which becomes Farm Security Administration
1941	receives Guggenheim Foundation grant
1942	photographs Japanese internment camps
1958	travels around the world
OCTOBER 11, 1965	Lange dies in Berkeley, California
1966	"Dorothea Lange Retrospective" opens at the Museum of Modern Art

Further Reading

Meltzer, Milton. *Dorothea Lange: A Photographer's Life.* New York: Farrar, Straus & Giroux, 1978. An excellent, thoroughly researched adult biography.

_____. *Dorothea Lange: Life Through the Camera.* New York: Viking Kestrel, 1985. Shorter version of the biography, for young readers.

Ohrn, Karin Becker. *Dorothea Lange and the Documentary Tradition.* Baton Rouge: Louisiana State University Press, 1980. In-depth look at 1930s photography and Lange's life.

Stryker, Roy Emerson, and Nancy Wood. *In This Proud Land.* Greenwich, Conn.: New York Graphic Society, 1973. Filled with Lange photographs and those of other government photographers of the 1935–1943 era.

Margaret Bourke-White

(1904–1971)

When Margaret Bourke-White asked for permission to photograph inside a steel mill, she was told women weren't allowed.
So she went to the top. Through contacts she had made from
photography assignments, she met Elroy Kulas, the president of Otis
Steel, one of the largest steel manufacturers in the United States. He
was so taken by her intense interest that he told his management she
was permitted to take whatever photographs she wanted.

Bourke-White had not anticipated how difficult it would be. The
mill was dark; the only light radiated from the molten metal and that
light showed poorly on the film available to her. Night after night,
she returned to the mill. She brought two friends, a camera shop

Margaret Bourke-White, *1929, photographer unknown. Bourke-White climbed out on
scaffolding 800 feet in the air when she was hired to take photos of the construction of
the Chrysler Building in New York, and yet the building's management wouldn't lease
her space for a studio because she was a woman. She persisted and got the studio.*
(Margaret Bourke-White Papers, Syracuse University Library, Department of Special Collections;
Courtesy Bourke-White Estate)

owner and a photofinisher. They lugged in heavy equipment and tried every camera and lens they had. They brought in floodlights, laid cables, and set off flashpans. She took her equipment in so close to the heat that the varnish blistered on the wooden camera. But she couldn't get a good photograph.

Finally, they made contact with a salesman on his way to Hollywood. He had magnesium flares for the motion picture industry. When all the equipment had been set up, the flares were ignited for 30 seconds to allow time for eight-second, four-second, and two-second exposures to capture what Bourke-White envisioned: "That last spectacular moment in the pouring of the ingot molds—that dramatic moment when the columns of tall tubular forms are full to bursting, each crowned with a fiery corona of sparks, and the cooling ladle in one last effort empties the final drops of its fiery load and turns away."

At the age of 23, Margaret Bourke-White had made a breakthrough in the science of photography and in the reporting of an era. The president of Otis Steel bought eight photographs at $100 each and published them in a stockholders' report, *The Story of Steel*. Within two weeks, a selection of her photographs ran in several Midwestern newspapers and she received offers to create advertising photographs for Chrysler Motors and Republic Steel.

"It is odd that photography was never one of my childhood hobbies when Father was so fond of it," Margaret Bourke-White wrote in her autobiography. "I hardly touched a camera and certainly never operated one until after he died."

Yet as a child, she loved to watch her father, Joseph White, tinker with the lenses he invented and patented. She was thrilled when she could look through the prisms and ground glass to see the magic effects of illusion.

After her birth on June 14, 1904, in the Bronx, New York, Margaret Bourke White (she later added the hyphen) was raised in Bound Brook, New Jersey, with a brother and sister.

At an early age, Peggy—as she was called, and later, Maggie—imagined herself "going to the jungle, bringing back specimens for natural history museums and doing all the things that women never do." She hiked through the woodlands and collected snakes, turtles, and insects, which she kept in cages and jars around the house.

The Whites encouraged their children to be independent, but they were protective. They restricted socializing with other children after school, and they maintained strict, old-fashioned discipline. Maggie turned to activities within the family, especially her father's construction of gadgets and machinery.

What intrigued her most about his work were the trips to the factories where he supervised the installation of printing presses he invented. She recalled her first visit to a foundry where she climbed up a sooty balcony to wait for a rush of flowing metal and flying sparks that broke the darkness. "To me at that age," she said, "a foundry represented the beginning and end of all beauty."

Unfortunately, when Margaret was 17 years old, her father died suddenly and left the family with little money. She became an art student after high school and enrolled in Columbia University, where she took a course in photography. Her mother gave her a secondhand camera.

The course was given by Clarence White, who had been one of Alfred Stieglitz's Photo-Secessionists. He produced soft-focus, romantic photographs in high contrast of lights and shadows. Bourke-White's first photographs were in this pictorial style.

Margaret Bourke-White had to rely on scholarships and a benefactor to pay her way through college. She left Columbia for a series of five other colleges, where she studied biology. At Purdue University, 1924 she married Everett Chapman, a doctoral candidate and scientist. But the marriage didn't work out and she returned to Cleveland, where her family was living. She was divorced later.

Throughout her college years, Bourke-White earned money by selling photographs of students, campuses, and surrounding countrysides. She became particularly interested in taking photographs of buildings. In 1927 as she finished her last semester at Cornell University in Ithaca, New York, she went to New York City during Easter vacation. She took her portfolio of photographs and walked

Molten Slag Overflows from Ladle, Otis Steel Co., c. 1927-28, by Margaret Bourke-White. Her experiments with photography inside a steel mill led to Bourke-White becoming America's most visible industrial photographer. (Margaret Bourke-White Papers, Syracuse University Library, Department of Special Collections; Courtesy Bourke-White Estate)

into an architectural firm without an appointment. An architect there took such an interest in her work that she was encouraged to pursue photography as a profession.

After graduation, she returned to Cleveland. On the night boat from Buffalo, she reflected, "As the skyline took form in the early morning mist, I felt I was coming to my promised land: columns of masonry gaining height as we drew toward the pier, derricks swinging like living creatures—deep inside I knew these were my subjects."

With great determination, Bourke-White pursued leads from associates and presented her portfolio to firms in Cleveland. Soon she began selling many architectural and garden scenes to private companies, building owners, and local magazines. She converted her apartment into a darkroom. Working at night, she developed photos in the kitchen sink, processed them in the kitchenette, and rinsed them in the bathtub.

In her free time, she haunted the commercial sections of town, where she photographed trestles, railroads, concrete, and steel. Whenever she could, she got into factories to shoot turbines, gears, wheels—the action of the machine age. Just as she had been delighted to see the workings of a foundry when she was young, she felt that industrial forms were close to her heart.

After the triumph of her steel mill photographs, Henry Luce, the publisher of the six-year-old *Time* magazine, cabled her to come to New York. Luce was developing *Fortune,* an illustrated magazine of business and industry. Bourke-White worked for *Fortune* six months a year for the next six years.

In 1930, Bourke-White moved to New York City. She took a studio at the Chrysler Building, which she had photographed earlier that year. Often in subfreezing temperatures, she had ascended 800 feet above the street to an open scaffold, where she set up her equipment in a tower that swayed up to eight feet in the wind.

In the 1930s, mass production held the promise of accessible products and an easier, more convenient life. Traveling constantly for *Fortune,* Bourke-White photographed shoemaking, orchid raising, meat packing, and Atlantic coast fisheries. She shot bottles, paper, aluminum, and chewing gum. Using dramatic angles, she captured the action of industry and turned it into heroic proportions.

Gargoyle on the Chrysler Building, *1930, by Margaret Bourke-White. The steel gargoyle was a perfect symbol of the Bourke-White vision, which championed the power of
industry. Inside, her studio was finished in sleek Art Deco design and housed her pet alli-
gators and turtles.* (Margaret Bourke-White Papers, Syracuse University Library, Department of
Special Collections; Courtesy Bourke-White Estate)

The distinct, sharp images of her prints displayed the beauty of metal, leather, glass, and cement.

Bourke-White also traveled to Europe. She was especially keen to photograph the Soviet Union, but it had been closed to western photographers since after World War I. Above all, Margaret Bourke-White hated closed doors. She persevered and finally was allowed into the country. She made a 5,000-mile trip to photograph the machine age and wrote a book about her experiences, *Eyes on Russia.*

During the 1930s, Bourke-White operated a successful advertising photography studio. For her accounts, she photographed nail polish, soup, strawberry mousse, and even a knight in shining armor. For assignments for TWA and Eastern Airlines, she filled the seats with acquaintances, then flew strapped into a small aircraft in close formation with the big passenger plane.

Margaret Bourke-White enjoyed her role as star photographer. She bought expensive clothing and boldly wore slacks, an unusual fashion choice for women in the 1930s. She had little time for personal friendships and didn't remain close with family members. Yet, she attended important social events and always seemed to have a new man in her life.

Like everyone who read magazines and newspapers during the Great Depression, Bourke-White had seen the photographs taken by Dorothea Lange and other Farm Security Administration (FSA) photographers. In 1934, Bourke-White herself photographed the drought in the West.

By 1936, she was ready to aim her camera at new subjects and closed her advertising studio. "I began watching for the effect of events on human beings," she wrote. "I was awakening to the need of probing and learning, discovering and interpreting. I realized that any photographer who tries to portray human beings in a penetrating way must put more heart and mind into his preparation than will ever show in any photograph."

Fortune magazine publisher Henry Luce knew just how capable Bourke-White was. He sent her to Montana to photograph the construction of the Fort Peck Dam for a new magazine he was preparing to launch. She photographed the workers and went behind

> "Any photographer who tries to portray human beings in a penetrating way must put more heart and mind into his preparation than will ever show in any photograph."

the scenes to show how they lived in the boomtown formed by the construction site.

Bourke-White drew on a lineage of documentary photography. Mathew Brady had gone into battle to photograph the Civil War, and Lewis Hine had descended the coal mines to document working conditions. Although their photographs depicted people in true situations, the subjects were posed, mostly because of the limitations of film and camera equipment. Photographs taken by Dorothea Lange and others of the Farm Security Administration depicted people in more candid situations and created a more emotional appeal. These photos were used to illustrate articles or photo stories that presented strong visual images for a specific purpose. Hine's stories advocated child labor laws, and the FSA photographers showed the desperate situations of the Great Depression.

Margaret Bourke-White, Henry Luce, and the editors at *Life* perfected the magazine photo essay. Photos told the story and short, easy-to-read text filled in the details. Bourke-White helped define the image of *Life* magazine and many similar publications.

Her photograph of the monumental dam was on the cover of the first issue of *Life*, dated November 23, 1936. The magazine was an instant sellout and became America's premier publication, eventually reaching a circulation of 8 million readers.

"I woke up each morning ready for any surprise the day might bring," Bourke-White wrote. "I loved the swift pace of the *Life* assignments, the exhilaration of stepping over the threshold into a new land. Everything could be conquered. Nothing was too difficult. And if you had a stiff deadline to meet, all the better. You said yes to the challenge and shaped up the story accordingly, and found joy and a sense of accomplishment in so doing."

Margaret Bourke-White, known as the "girl photographer," became as famous as *Life*. Wherever she went she brought an entourage of assistants. Ralph Graves, a managing editor for the magazine, related an experience assisting her. "I never worked so hard in my life. . . . If lighting would improve a picture, out came the extension cords and the flashbulbs—in extravagant profusion. . . . If the picture looked good on one camera, she would try it again on two other cameras in case it looked better. And then again on still another camera in case it looked even better. . . . She said it was easy: they could all see how hard she was working, how much she wanted the perfect picture, and people were always willing to help that kind of determination."

On assignment to photograph the Arctic Circle, the plane and crew she chartered were forced to make an emergency landing at a remote village, where they stayed for two days until the weather cleared. While she was on assignment to uncover a story on child labor abuse in Jersey City, she was chased, captured, and briefly jailed by the mayor's henchmen, but first had managed to slip the roll of exposed film into safe hands.

She accepted an offer to take photographs for a book authored by Erskine Caldwell, a best-selling author and playwright. They traveled together throughout the South the summer of 1936. Bourke-White photographed sharecroppers and chain gangs to illustrate their book, *You Have Seen Their Faces*. Margaret Bourke-White and Erskine Caldwell became a celebrated couple constantly noted by the press. They were married a few years later, in 1939.

In 1938, she was assigned to travel to Czechoslovakia, a hotbed of changing political loyalties. She arranged the trip with Caldwell, who researched and wrote the text for their second collaboration, *North of the Danube*. They witnessed the growing power of the Third Reich. She photographed Nazi rallies and expanding arsenals.

During the early years of World War II, they went to Moscow. Bourke-White photographed the German bombing of the city and Caldwell wrote broadcasts, which he sent by radio every night. The marriage did not last, however, and they were divorced in 1942.

By the time the United States entered the war, Bourke-White became a war correspondent and a lieutenant in the air force. She wanted to photograph a bombing mission. Once again she heard a

Nazi Rally, Reichenberg, Bohemia, *1938, by Margaret Bourke-White. By the late 1930s, Bourke-White had turned her camera on human rights issues and photographed the dangerous buildup of military strength in Germany.* (Margaret Bourke-White Papers, Syracuse University Library, Department of Special Collections; Courtesy Bourke-White Estate)

familiar admonition: women weren't allowed. There was even an airplane named after her, but she couldn't fly in it.

She crossed from Europe to Africa in a boat crammed with military passengers. She didn't have enough room to bring everything; while she was packing, her glance fell upon her favorite lens. "It had photographed almost every famous person in the world," she later wrote, "Churchill, King George of England, Haile Selassie, Madam and the Generalissimo Chiang Kai-shek, Stalin, the Pope, Franklin D. Roosevelt. I threw the soap out and crammed the lens in."

The ship was torpedoed. The few minutes she spent waiting for the lifeboat were enough for her to recognize her own mortality, but not enough to dissuade her from taking pictures. As dawn cast its glance on the survivors at sea, she photographed them. Having survived a torpedoed ship was considered enough initiation—she was finally allowed to participate in combat.

Her most difficult task of the war came when she was in the lead group of General Patton's Third Army as it punched through Germany in the immediate wake of Nazi retreat. Bourke-White photographed terrified citizens, Nazi sympathizers who had killed themselves, and storehouses of food and treasures.

She also was one of the first liberators to enter Buchenwald, a concentration camp near Weimar, Germany. She photographed charred bodies piled high and desperate prisoners clinging to life. The war changed her. She said, "I come away from what I have been photographing sick at heart, with the faces of people in pain etched as sharply in my mind as on my negatives. But I go back because I feel it is my place to make such pictures."

It was not the last time her camera photographed human atrocities. In the summer of 1946 she traveled to India. The country was preparing for its independence from the colonial rule of Great Britain. Mohandas Gandhi, the great peacekeeper known as the Mahatma, or great one, wanted a unified nation. But leaders of the Muslim religion wanted their own country, and Pakistan was carved from the north of India.

More than five million people exchanged countries. Hindus had to leave the area of Pakistan, giving up their homes and their land. Muslims left their homes in India to move to Pakistan. Centuries of conflict peaked, and the two sides fought. Riots spread and hundreds of thousands of people were murdered.

Bourke-White photographed the partition and the great leaders of India. She also lived at Gandhi's ashram while she researched. In order to photograph Gandhi, she was required to learn how to spin wool by hand. "Photography demands a high degree of participation," she wrote, "but never have I participated to such an extent as I did

"*Utter truth is essential and that is what stirs me when I look through the camera.*"

when photographing various episodes in the life of Gandhi." In response, Gandhi affectionately called her the "torturer." One morning she interviewed him and he expressed his commitment to peace. He was assassinated later that day. From her experiences in India, she wrote *Halfway to Freedom.*

When she was not on assignment, Bourke-White lived in Connecticut. Throughout her career she had set aside time to photograph such phenomena as praying mantises hatching from eggs or butterflies completing metamorphosis. She still collected insects found in the woods surrounding her house and except for times during snowbound winters, she slept and worked outdoors.

She continued traveling the globe. In 1950 she went to South Africa to document mining operations. She photographed the miners performing traditional dances in the evenings. During the day she traveled over a mile below ground where the atmosphere was so stifling she could not speak and barely managed to operate her equipment.

As the police action escalated in South Korea, Bourke-White wanted to get back into a war zone. There, she lived with South Korean communist guerrillas to get true-to-life photographs of their activities in the hills.

Soon after Korea, she became aware that she was losing motor control in her limbs. She stumbled, dropped things, or suddenly jerked her arm. To her, this behavior was shocking. "The strong might fall by the wayside," she said, "But I was indestructible." She was diagnosed with Parkinson's disease.

The illness would get worse. But Bourke-White exercised her hands and walked every day to keep her strength.

As she had imagined herself years before, she got her chance to explore the South American jungle, where she photographed American Jesuit missions. She continued to take *Life* assignments, although she rested more in between.

Bourke-White underwent two separate brain operations to reverse the progress of the illness. Both times she ardently relearned motor control of her body. She practiced walking, stepping, throwing, typing. She gained enough strength to continue her camera work and to write her autobiography, *Portrait of Myself,* published in 1963.

Throughout her life she wrote seven books and collaborated with Caldwell on four more.

"I have always been glad I cast the die on the side I did," she wrote. "But a woman who lives a roving life must be able to stand alone. She must have emotional security, which is more important even than financial security. There is a richness in a life where you stand on your own two feet, although it imposes a certain creed. There must be no demands. Others have the right to be as free as you are. You must be able to take disappointments gallantly. You set your own ground rules, and if you follow them, there are great rewards."

After having traveled more than a million miles in 45 countries, Margaret Bourke-White reluctantly ended her career as a photographer and quietly lived in her Connecticut haven with a housekeeper. She fought Parkinson's for nearly 20 years, then died August 27, 1971.

Chronology

JUNE 14, 1904	Margaret Bourke-White born in the Bronx, New York
1906	moves to Bound Brook, New Jersey
1921	attends Columbia University, New York
1924	marries Everett Chapman
1927	receives degree from Cornell; moves to Cleveland; opens photography studio
1929	joins staff of *Fortune* magazine
1936	photographs *You Have Seen their Faces* with author Erskine Caldwell; joins staff of *Life* magazine
1938	travels to Europe
1939	marries Erskine Caldwell
1942	becomes first woman war correspondent
1943	becomes first woman to fly on a bombing mission with U.S. Air Force
1946	takes first trip to India; writes *Halfway to Freedom*
1952	covers Korean war
1959	undergoes treatment for Parkinson's disease
1963	publishes autobiography, *Portrait of Myself*
AUGUST 27, 1971	Bourke-White dies in Connecticut

Further Reading

Bourke-White's Books

Halfway to Freedom. New York; Simon and Schuster, 1949. Bourke-White's story of the partition of India.

Portrait of Myself. New York: Simon and Schuster, 1963. Bourke-White's autobiography.

Caldwell, Erskine, and Bourke-White, Margaret. *You Have Seen their Faces.* New York: The Viking Press, 1937. Bourke-White's photographs of the South.

Books About Margaret Bourke-White

Callahan, Sean. *The Photographs of Margaret Bourke-White.* Boston: New York Graphic Society, 1972. A good biography, well-illustrated.

Daffron, Carolyn. *Margaret Bourke-White.* New York: Chelsea House Publishers, 1988. An easy-to-read, young-adult biography.

Iverson, Genie. *Margaret Bourke-White: News Photographer.* Mankato, Minnesota: Creative Education, 1980. A children's biography.

Silverman, Jonathan. *For the World to See: The Life of Margaret Bourke-White.* New York: The Viking Press, 1983. A beautiful book of Bourke-White photographs, with accompanying biography.

Gordon Parks

(1912–   )

Gordon Parks was well-acquainted with prejudice and segregation when he grew up in Kansas and Minnesota. His first trip to Washington, D.C., in 1942, however, provided an intense exposure to a highly segregated society. During his first few days, he discovered that he couldn't eat at any lunch counter, wouldn't be waited on in any store, and was asked to use the rear entrance because the color of his skin was black.

The man who had brought Parks to the nation's capital, Roy Stryker, was in charge of the photographic division of the Farm Security Administration (FSA), the federal agency that provided loans to aid farmers, sharecroppers, and laborers. He warned Parks

Gordon Parks, *1946, by Morgan Smith. The youngest of 15 children raised in Kansas, Gordon Parks became a celebrated photographer, major motion picture director, musician, composer, and author.* (Courtesy Morgan Smith and the Photographs and Prints Division, Schomberg Center for Research in Black Culture, The New York Public Library, Astor, Lenox and Tilden Foundations)

111

about the difficulties he would encounter, but he also wanted to help him learn how the camera could expose prejudice.

Stryker pointed out a woman mopping the floor. He said, "Go have a talk with her before you go home this evening. See what she has to say about life and things."

Parks later recalled, "We started off awkwardly, neither of us knowing my reason for starting the conversation. At first it was a meaningless exchange of words. Then, as if a dam had broken within her, she began to spill out her life story. It was a pitiful one.

"She had struggled alone after her mother had died and her father had been killed by a lynch mob. She had gone through high school, married, and become pregnant. Her husband was accidentally shot to death two days before their daughter was born.

"By the time the daughter was eighteen she had given birth to two illegitimate children, dying two weeks after the second child's birth. What's more, the first child had been stricken with paralysis a year before its mother died. Now this woman was bringing up these grandchildren on a salary hardly suitable for one person."

Gordon Parks asked to photograph her and she replied, "I don't mind."

He posed her in front of a large American flag—the symbol of freedom—with the tools of one of the only trades a black woman could engage in.

"What the camera had to do," Parks said, "was expose the evils of racism, the evils of poverty, the discrimination and the bigotry, by showing the people who suffered most under it. That was the way it had to be done."

Later, he reflected, "The photograph of the black cleaning woman standing in front of the American flag with a broom and a mop expresses that more than any other photograph I have taken."

☆ ☆ ☆

Gordon Alexander Parks was born in Fort Scott, Kansas, on November 30, 1912. He loved growing up on the prairie, where he rode horses, fished, picked fruit from neighboring orchards, and enjoyed the wide open spaces. His father, Andrew Jackson Parks, was a farmer who was able to provide enough to eat and warm clothes for his 15 children. His mother, Sarah Ross Parks, was a cleaning woman who encouraged their children to get the best education they could. Gordon became an avid reader. From a young age, Gordon played piano and trombone and composed his own music. At school he became a good basketball player.

Gordon and his brothers and sisters attended a segregated school. There, they were told not to expect too much because few opportunities were open to educated black people. Gordon's mother, however, told him, "If a white boy can do it, so can you. Don't ever come home telling me you couldn't do this or that because you're black." He used that as a guide his entire life.

Gordon's mother died in 1928, just before he was 16, and he went to live with a sister and her husband in St. Paul, Minnesota. But his brother-in-law didn't like him and threw him out of the house. Determined to get his high school diploma, Gordon went to school during the day and rode the trolleys all night so he could be somewhere warm. Although he tried to finish school, he finally quit because he had to work.

Jobs for a black young adult were limited—even more so after the stock-market crash of 1929 and the beginning of the Great Depression. But Gordon Parks was willing to work hard. He mopped floors in a dirty flophouse, played piano in a bar, worked as a bellboy, and eventually got a job as a busboy at a hotel that hosted big bands on tour. During off hours, he played his own songs at the piano. One visiting bandleader liked his song "No Love" so much, that he orchestrated it and it was played at the hotel and on national radio. Another visiting bandleader invited him to tour. But the band broke up just as it arrived in New York.

Parks joined the Civilian Conservation Corps, a government-sponsored program for beautifying national parks and recreation areas. In 1933, while he was stationed in Fort Dix, New Jersey, he married Sally Alvis. They would have three children, Gordon, Toni, and David.

They moved to Minneapolis, Minnesota, and Parks took a series of jobs, including a position as a semiprofessional basketball player. To support his growing family, Parks became a railroad dining car waiter, where he interacted with a wide variety of people from all classes and occupations. He read the magazines passengers left on the train and especially studied the photographs—both fashion and the news.

He was particularly impressed with the photographs of Dorothea Lange, Ben Shahn, and other Depression-era photographers. Parks later wrote, "These stark images of men, women, and children, caught in their confusion and poverty, saddened me."

During one trip to Chicago, in 1937, Parks went to an afternoon movie. He watched a newsreel of Japanese war planes bombing a U.S. ship. The photographer had put his life in danger to photograph the horror of the war. Surprisingly, the photographer was in the audience and got up on stage while the audience cheered him. It was then, Parks later wrote, that he made up his mind to be a photographer.

Soon he bought himself a secondhand camera. He took thousands of photographs and read everything he could about photography. A few of his photos were published in local newspapers.

To make a living as a photographer, Parks decided to pursue fashion photography. He went to every large department store in the Minneapolis-St. Paul area and asked to photograph their merchandise. Most of the stores, including Frank Murphy's, had their fashions photographed in Chicago. But Mrs. Murphy was impressed with Gordon Parks and set up a photo shoot for the next night.

Once he got the assignment, he had to scramble to borrow the right equipment and quickly learn how to use it. Mrs. Murphy watched how Parks set up the models and lights and gave him another assignment, to take photographs at a country club. But that night as he developed the film, he realized he had double-exposed every shot but one. Nevertheless, he enlarged it, framed it, and showed it to Mrs. Murphy. She liked it enough to give him another chance.

Parks continued to do freelance photography while he worked for the railroad. With a wife and a young family, he needed the steady income. But in 1940 he was offered a fully equipped darkroom in Chicago in exchange for photographing events and exhibitions at the Southside Community Art Center. Determined to be successful as a full-time photographer, he moved his family to Chicago. He developed a steady clientele and earned a modest income. The art center gave him an exhibition.

Union Station, *1942*, *by Gordon Parks. Diverse architectural elements decorate the Washington, D.C., train station during World War II. After fighting for liberty in Europe, America focused on equality at home.* (Library of Congress)

While he wasn't working on photo shoots, Parks took his camera out in the city. Although he saw wealth and industry, he was more intrigued with the struggles of the poor. He thought about the FSA photographers. "It suddenly occurred to me that those guys were doing something with pictures that maybe I would want to do, too," he said. "They were photographing poverty, and I knew poverty so well."

In 1941 he applied for and received a fellowship from the Julius Rosenwald Fund, the first photographer to receive the award. Parks knew just what he would do with the $200-a-month fellowship—become an FSA photographer. Stryker accepted him and Parks moved to Washington, D.C. Stryker was criticized for engaging a black person, and Parks had to contend with harassment from whites and blacks, when, for example, he refused to sit in the black section of the lunchroom. He eventually won the respect of the white technicians who developed and printed his photographs.

Because of the United States involvement in World War II, Stryker moved to the Office of War Information. He offered Parks one of the few positions as staff photographer. Again, Parks was the only black person on the team.

During World War II, the United States armed forces were segregated. Parks spent time with an all-black squadron of air force pilots training for bombing raids into Nazi Germany. He was all set to go with them, but suddenly his orders changed. No official explanation ever came regarding why Parks could not photograph the all-black company in action.

In 1944, Roy Stryker continued to employ Parks when he went to work for the Standard Oil Company. Standard Oil had been the target of reformers 30 years earlier, when Lewis Hine was taking photographs to pass child labor laws. Articles about Standard Oil had disclosed the company's strong-arm tactics to get people to cooperate. But in the decades since, Standard Oil and its director, John D. Rockefeller, Jr., tried to change the company's image as one that supported charities and the common worker. The company hired photographers to create a pictorial record of the home front. Parks moved to New York to be close to the Standard Oil headquarters. He published two books on photographic techniques.

To boost his freelance income, Parks took his portfolio to magazines. *Harper's Bazaar* was a popular publication that used fashion photography. But the Hearst organization did not hire black people. Roy Stryker suggested that Parks go see the photographer Edward Steichen. Steichen at that time had retired from his successful career

Cleaning a Drum, Pittsburgh, *1944, by Gordon Parks. As a staff photographer for Standard Oil, Parks photographed strength and pride in a worker lifting a drum from a solution of boiling lye.* (Standard Oil of New Jersey Collection, University of Louisville Photographic Archives)

GORDON PARKS

as a fashion and celebrity photographer. He sent Parks to the editor of *Vogue* magazine, who gave Parks assignments.

In 1949, Parks showed his portfolio to *Life*'s picture editor. The magazine was regarded as the biggest and the best of the photo-essay publications. *Life* photographers and writers got first-class treatment and exclusive stories. They were paid well and all expenses were covered. After looking at his portfolio, the editor asked Parks what he would like to photograph if he got an assignment. A Harlem gang leader, Parks blurted out.

He walked out with the assignment but realized he hadn't planned what he would do. Through the police station, he made contact with a gang leader. Being black gave him a certain opening, but he had to earn trust. He went everywhere with the gang for a few days, then finally started taking photos. His photographs on gang life and turf wars broke new ground for the magazine. Parks became the first black staff photographer for *Life* magazine.

Because he had done fashion photography, Parks was assigned to the Paris bureau, where he spent two years. Parks thoroughly enjoyed European life. No "whites only" signs hung on the doors of establishments and he felt his color was not as important as in America. But he believed that the United States, though more prejudiced, offered more opportunities for him and his children.

From 1950 to 1970, five million black people moved from rural areas into central cities of the United States. Black servicemen returning from the war were still being asked to use segregated facilities and rear entrances after they had endangered their lives for the country. In 1955, Rosa Parks spurred a revolt when she refused to give up her bus seat to a white passenger, as the law required. Her arrest brought Dr. Martin Luther King, Jr., to national prominence. Muhammad Ali, the heavyweight champion, and Malcolm X, a political leader, spoke out against racism in America. Gordon Parks photographed them all.

Parks also photographed the Black Panthers, a militant organization. He rode with the leaders as they were followed by the police. When he was asked to join them, he said, "Well, you know, I'm in the fight the same as you are. I ride with you every night. You have chosen a gun; I have chosen a camera . . . I think my weapon is stronger." In 1961, Parks traveled to Brazil. He chose to focus on the life of Flavio, a dying boy and his family living in a filthy slum. During the time spent with the family, Parks had grown attached to them. Although he brought them bags of groceries, he couldn't personally do much to change the course of their lives. Professionally, however, his *Life* story of Flavio was so well received that thousands of people sent money to bring Flavio to the United States for medical care. His family was given a house, and the boy returned healthy to his native country.

"*I*'m in the same fight as you [Black Panthers] are. You have chosen a gun; I have chosen a camera. . . . I think my weapon is stronger.*"*

Although his photographs of black leaders and situations of poverty are some of his most powerful, Parks covered all types of stories from the ballet and art exhibitions to hurricanes and hospitals. The public was fascinated with the private lives of celebrities, politicians, royalty, and other public figures. He photographed British prime minister Winston Churchill, poet Robert Frost, actors Paul Newman and Joanne Woodward, artist Alexander Calder, and boxer Sugar Ray Leonard. Parks was a *Life* staff photographer until 1969 and after that continued to have his work published as a freelancer.

During his long journey from hunger to fame, Parks reflected on his origins and influences. He wrote, "I believe my advantage was the great love of my family—seven boys and eight girls, and a mother and father who cared about me. A lot of black kids in cities and rural areas don't even know who their mothers or fathers are. Life is a whole different thing for them."

He wrote *The Learning Tree,* a book about his life growing up black in Kansas. It became a best-seller. Later, he wrote three other autobiographies, five volumes of poetry and photographs, and two novels. In 1970 he was a founder of *Essence* magazine and served as the publication's editorial director for three years. He also wrote articles, poetry, and essays for other magazines, and went through his

American Gothic, *1942, by Gordon Parks. This straight-on shot of Ella Watson carries the message that not all people are protected by liberty and justice, represented by the American flag on the wall.* (Library of Congress)

vast collection of negatives to produce exhibitions for museums and galleries.

By the early 1960s, Gordon Parks and his wife had grown apart. They divorced, and Parks married Elizabeth Campbell; together they had one child, Leslie.

The 1960s also brought Parks to another career—making films. His first films were documentaries—one about Flavio and one about a Harlem family. He was offered his first Hollywood project to film his book, *The Learning Tree*, for which he also wrote the screenplay and the musical score.

"Just remembering that no black had been given a chance to direct a motion picture in Hollywood since it was established kept me going," he later wrote. "No day was free of problems, but somewhere there were answers, and I lay awake late into the nights searching for them."

From 1968 through 1976, Parks wrote and directed four other films, including the blockbuster *Shaft,* about a black private detective; *Shaft's Big Score; The Super Cops;* and *Leadbelly,* about blues musician Huddie Ledbetter. He also directed a television movie about a freeman who was illegally enslaved. In each of the films, many of the artists and film crew were black.

Parallel to his remarkable careers in photography and film, Parks evolved as a distinguished composer. His first piano concerto was performed in 1955, in Venice, Italy. Along with film scores and popular music, he wrote sonatas and a symphony. His ballet about the life of Martin Luther King, Jr., *Martin,* premiered in Washington, D.C., and Parks made a film version in 1989.

A life of travel and creative pursuits tends to strain family relationships. Parks was married for a third time, in 1973, to Genevieve Young. By this time, Parks had established a large extended family, which eventually included grandchildren and great-grandchildren.

"I have learned a few things along the way," he wrote. "The lesson I value most is to take human beings as they are, to take the measure of them; to accept or reject them, regardless of their wealth, impoverishment or color."

Through determination and talent, Gordon Parks broke through color barriers and has inspired young artists. He has received 28 honorary degrees in literature, fine arts, and humane letters from colleges and universities across America. In 1972 he received the prestigious Springarn Medal from the Na-

"*What the camera had to do was expose the evils of racism . . . by showing the people who suffered the most under it. That was the way it had to be done.*"

tional Association for the Advancement of Colored People (NAACP), and in 1988 he received the National Medal of Arts from President Ronald Reagan.

During the 1990s, he published *Voices in the Mirror,* an autobiography, and *Arias in Silence,* a book of poetry and color photography that depict the abstract forms of such natural objects as leaves and flowers. Exhibitions of his photographs continue to tour the United States.

"Success is filled with the agony of how and why—in the flesh, nerves and conscience," Parks wrote. "It takes you down a lonely road and you feel, at times, that you are traveling it alone. You can only keep walking. During that loneliness you get to know who you are."

Chronology

NOVEMBER 30, 1912	Gordon Parks born in Fort Scott, Kansas
1928	moves to St. Paul, Minnesota
1932	has his song "No Love" performed on national radio
1933	marries Sally Alvis
1938	starts fashion photography
1941	receives fellowship from the Julius Rosenwald Fund
1942	works for photographic division of Farm Security administration, then Office of War Information
1944	works as staff photographer for Standard Oil
1949	works as staff photographer for *Life* magazine
1955	attends premier performance of his first piano concerto
1963	marries Elizabeth Campbell, publishes *The Learning Tree*
1966	publishes *A Choice of Weapons*
1968	produces, directs, writes, and composes score for the movie version of *The Learning Tree*
1971	directs the movie *Shaft*
1973	marries Genevieve Young
1975	directs the movie *Leadbelly*
1988	receives the National Medal of Arts from President Ronald Reagan
1989	directs the film of his ballet, *Martin*
1994	publishes *Arias in Silence*

Further Reading

Parks's Books
Growing Up Black: From Slave Days to the Present. New York: Avon Books, 1992. Twenty-five African-americans reveal the trials and triumphs of their childhoods.
A Choice of Weapons. New York: Harper and Row, 1966. Compelling autobiography from childhood through war years.
The Learning Tree. New York: Harper and Row, 1963. Novel of growing up black in Kansas.
To Smile in Autumn. New York: Norton, 1979. Autobiography covering whole life.
Voices in the Mirror. New York: Doubleday, 1990. Autobiography from war to later years.
Arias in Silence. New York: Bullfinch Press, 1994. Poems and color photographs.

Video by Parks
Visions: The Images, Words and Music of Gordon Parks. New York: Past America Inc., Xenon Home Video, distributed by Modern Educational Video Network, 1986. Parks presents his life through his art.

Books About Gordon Parks
Berry, Skip. *Gordon Parks.* New York: Chelsea House Publishers, 1991. An easy-to-read young adult biography of Parks illustrated with his photographs.
Bush, Martin H. *The Photographs of Gordon Parks.* Wichita, Kansas: Wichita State University, 1983. An interview with Gordon Parks, illustrated with his photographs.
Turk, Midge. *Gordon Parks.* New York: Thomas Y. Crowell Company, 1971. An easy-to-read children's biography, illustrated with drawings.

About the Photographs

The photographs in this book were reproduced with permission from the following sources:

MATHEW B. BRADY

page x   *Mathew B. Brady*, photo by Levin Corbin Handy, 1875
Library of Congress, Washington, D.C., Negative No.:
LC-BH826-2681

page 5   *Edward, Prince of Wales*, 1860
Library of Congress, Washington, D.C., Negative No.:
LC-BH821-749

page 9   *M. B. Brady's New Photographic Gallery, Corner of Broadway and Tenth Street, New York*, engraving by A. Berghaus, 1861
Library of Congress, Washington, D.C., Negative No.:
LC-Z62-31052

page 12   *Cooper Union Portrait of Abraham Lincoln*, 1860
Library of Congress, Washington, D.C., Negative No.:
LC-BH8277

EDWARD S. CURTIS

page 16   *Self-Portrait*, 1899
Special Collections Division, University of Washington

ALFRED STIEGLITZ

LEWIS W. HINE

DOROTHEA LANGE

MARGARET BOURKE-WHITE

GORDON PARKS

Index

Boldface numbers indicate main topics. *Italic* page numbers indicate illustrations or captions.

PHOTOGRAPHERS